Landscapes of the
COSTA BLANCA

a countryside guide
Fourth edition

John and Christine Oldfield

Fourth edition © 2009
Sunflower Books™
PO Box 36160
London SW7 3WS, UK
www.sunflowerbooks.co.uk

Sunflower Books and
'Landscapes' are
Registered Trademarks

ISBN 978-1-85691-364-5

Well at Caprala (Walk 24)

Important note to the reader

We have tried to ensure that the descriptions and maps in this book are
error-free at press date. The book will be updated, where necessary,
whenever future printings permit. It will be very helpful for us to receive
your comments (sent in care of the publishers, please) for the updating
of future printings.

   We also rely on those who use this book — especially walkers —
to take along a good supply of common sense when they explore.
Conditions change fairly rapidly in these mountains, and ***storm damage
or bulldozing may make a route unsafe at any time***. If the route is not
as we outline it here, and your way ahead is not secure, return to the
point of departure. ***Never attempt to complete a tour or walk under
hazardous conditions!*** Please read carefully the notes on pages 39 to
44, as well as the introductory comments at the beginning of each tour
and walk (regarding road conditions, equipment, grade, distances and
time, etc). Explore ***safely***, while at the same time respecting the beauty
of the countryside.

Cover p...
Title pa...   *lmond
blosso...*

Photogr...
Maps b...   panish
militar...   co del
Ejércit...
A CIP ca...   ibrary.
Printed...

10 9 8 7...

☀ Contents _____

4 Landscapes of the Costa Blanca

Cherry orchards near L'Orxa, with Benicadell rising in the distance (Car tour 2)

Preface

The pleasure of researching and writing the First edition of this book in 1995/6 has been amply rewarded over the years by the warm and constructive correspondence we have received from users. We no longer live in Spain, but always enjoy returning to the mountains and valleys of the Costa Blanca, checking the walks and exploring different routes. On these return visits, we regularly meet and chat with people using the guide and grasp every opportunity to hear first hand about any changes and suggestions for new routes.

Several of the changes incorporated in this Fourth edition have come from such suggestions, and we believe they make this an even better edition. A number of walks have been re-routed to take into account new roads and the increasing trend for the local councils to create new walking routes, as more people are beginning to realise the incredible beauty of this region. In addition, we have been able to include several new alternative walks, some of which follow old trails upgraded thanks to EU funding. Signposting and waymarking has improved beyond all measure in the last few years.

So make the most of the mountains, castles and valleys of this hospitable and spectacular area. And carry your *Landscapes* book visibly — you never know, the couple you pass next time may be us!

Acknowledgements

The original book was written with the invaluable assistance of the Centro Excursionista de Valencia, Rafael Cebrián, Eric Wright and Ross Gow. Subsequent editions owe much to the many users who have taken the time to contact us via Sunflower Books. Their constructive suggestions, advice and ideas have been incorporated where appropriate in order to make this a more accurate and up-to-date guide.

Language, place names and glossary

Many people on the tourist beat speak English, but that is not the case when you leave the coast. A simple Spanish phrase book or pocket dictionary can be invaluable — although many older people speak Valenciano and are uncomfortable with Spanish.

In the Costa Blanca region you will quickly become aware that place names may have two different spellings — **Castellano** (Spanish as we know it) and **Valenciano**. Mostly the two are very similar, with just an omitted letter or added accent, but in a few cases they can be quite different, for example Jávea becomes Xábia, Jijona Xixona. The

Serra de Aitana

revival of Valenciano means that Castilian names are gradually being phased out, but some towns and features are still known by their Castilian names. In this book we use the version you are most likely to encounter, but give both versions where confusion might occur.

SNOW WELLS *(casas de nieve, neveras, pous, cavas, cavetas)*

Several of our walks feature well-preserved *pous* or *cavas*, and you will be amazed by their size and the solidity of their construction.

Before the days of the refrigerator, snow was commercially 'harvested', compacted in a well and left till summer, when it was cut into blocks of ice. During the coolest time of the day, usually in the hours of darkness, the ice was transported down the mountains by mule, donkey or cart,

to the distant towns. These wells are described by different names, depending on their location — for example those on the Carrasqueta Ridge are called *pous*, while those around Agres are called *cavas*.

High in the mountains, walls were built in strategic locations to catch the drifting snow and, whenever there had been a significant fall, men would be hired to shovel it into a *pou* and press it down. These *pous* were sometimes just natural dips in the ground but, more often, were

Preface

Some of the older settlements have rather long names, but it customary to abbreviate them. We have used full names once only. For instance, after mentioning Planes de la Baronía, we refer to it thereafter simply as Planes. There are many place names beginning with 'Beni', for example Bienialí, Benirrama, Benitaia. These are relics of the Moorish occupation, the prefix being comparable to the Scottish 'Mac'.

In the course of the text, where it 'felt right', we have used some local words instead of the English equivalent. In the glossary below we give their meaning.

ambiente atmosphere
arroyo stream
autovía dual carriageway
ayuntamiento, ajuntament town hall
barra French stick, baguette
barranco, barranc gorge, ravine, gully
bocadillo sandwich (often half a *barra*)
bodega wine cellar/shop
cabo, cap cape
calle, carrer street
camino, camí small street, path
camino rural country road
canaleta small water channel
casa/casita house/little house
castillo, castell castle
cava/caveta snow well (see below)
cerro hill
coll, collado hill or saddle
corral farm
correos post office
coto privado de caza private hunting reserve
cueva, cova cave
embalse, presa reservoir
ermita hermitage or chapel
finca farmhouse and farm

fuente, font spring
gasoleo diesel
gasolina petrol
hostal cheap hotel
hoya, foia valley, basin
huerta market garden
lavadero wash-house
levante east
masía, mas farm
mirador viewpoint
molino, molí windmill
nao ship
nevera snow well (see below)
peña, penya rock
piscina swimming pool
playa, platja beach
plaza square
puerto, port mountain pass (or seaport)
pou snow well (see below)
puig mountain
río, riu river
salinas saltpans
santuario, santuari sanctuary or hermitage
tapas snacks or appetizers
torrente dry river bed
turrón almond sweetmeat
valle, vall valley
vuelta circuit

specially constructed for the purpose. Pits were dug, usually cylindrical in form, and when full of snow were covered with brushwood and branches to ward off the worst of the summer heat. More sophisticated wells were covered by a stone hut with a conical roof and two or three access doors. Stone steps or iron rungs would be set into the walls of the pit to enable the pressers and block-cutters to get down to the snow level, and special tools were used to the blocks.

Caveta del Buitre (Walk 19)

❀ Getting about

There is a reasonable bus service between the main centres on the coast and some of the larger inland towns, but in the mountain regions bus times are not designed to suit walkers. However, it is possible to reach some of our walks by **bus**, and we have included the relevant timetables on pages 133-134. Timetables can vary, depending on the season, so visit local bus stations for up-to-date information (tourist offices in this area do not usually keep bus timetables). A few walks are also accessible by **train** or by El Trenet (timetable page 133). El Trenet (sometimes called El Limonero or the 'Lemon Express') runs up and down the coast between Dénia and Alicante, stopping at every imaginable place en route and affording leisurely views of coastline and countryside. For some of the walks you could make use of a **taxi**, or arrange to stay overnight close to the area where they start.

The most practical option is to **hire a car**. This way you are free to stop at will to admire a view, fill up water bottles at roadside *fonts,* or explore some of the fascinating villages through which you will pass. Cars can be hired at reasonable prices through travel firms when booking flights. Alternatively, in the coastal towns, there are many companies vying for business with special offers and discounts. Make sure you know exactly what you are paying for before hiring; the price quoted may not include collision damage waiver or unlimited mileage.

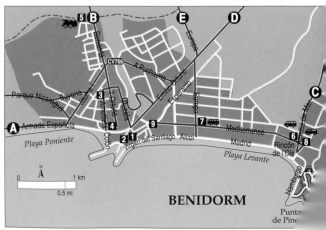

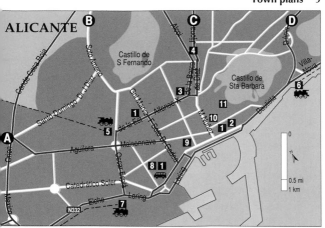

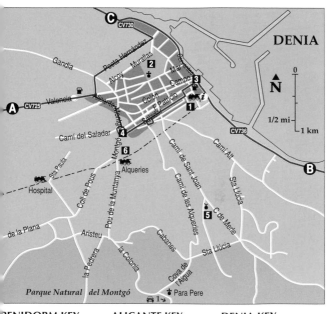

BENIDORM KEY
1. Tourist office
2. Town hall
3. Police
4. Market
5. Railway station
6. Albir buses
7. ALSA buses
8. Guadalest buses
9. Plaza de la Hispanidad

ALICANTE KEY
1. Tourist offices
2. Town hall
3. Market
4. Street market
5. RENFE railway station
6. FGV railway station
7. Murcia railway station
8. Bus station
9. Post office
10. Cathedral
11. Museum

DENIA KEY
1. Railway station and tourist information
2. Dénia castle
3. Cruz Roja (Red Cross)
4. MAPFRE roundabout
5. Mosque
6. Alqueries station

❀ Picnicking

We have found some spectacular picnic spots during our walks through the mountains in this area of Spain. They should appeal to those who prefer *very* short walks. If you are car touring, they are an 'off-the-beaten-track' alternative to the area's designated picnic sites, mostly by the roadside, with benches and bins (indicated in the touring notes with the symbol ⊼). These tend to get quite busy on Sundays and *fiestas*. How much better it is to get away from the trappings of civilisation and enjoy a picnic in the wilderness, watching a stream flow by, admiring a mountain view or listening to the birds!

All the information you need to find these more secluded picnic spots is given below, where *picnic numbers correspond to walk numbers,* so you can quickly find their general location by looking at the touring map (where walks are outlined in white). We give you walking times and transport details. The precise location of the picnic spot is indicated by the symbol *P* on the appropriate *walking map,* which also shows the nearest 🚗 parking place and 🚌 stop (if accessible by bus).

Please remember to **wear sensible shoes** and **take a sunhat**. It's a good idea to take a plastic groundsheet as well, in case it's damp or prickly.

Take food *with you* for picnics; don't rely on buying it en route. There are few shops in the villages, and their range is quite limited. A fresh *barra*, a hunk of cheese, a couple of tomatoes and some fresh fruit make a satisfying feast. We always carry a small sharp knife, salt and serviettes, to avoid making up sandwiches in advance.

At some of the picnic sites there are *fonts*, so you can enjoy a refreshing cool drink with your food and refill your water bottles. But after long droughts and in the height of summer some *fonts* might run dry; do not *rely* on them as your only source of liquid on a trip. And, of course, leave no rubbish behind, even if others have done so before you.

All picnickers should heed the country code on the facing page.

Right: Montgó from the highest point on Cap Prim (Walk 2c — and just a short stroll from the setting for Picnic 2c)

A country code for walkers, motorists and picnickers

The Spanish countryside is essentially unspoiled. It is only around the more accessible, and therefore popular, picnic or camping areas that you will come across litter. Please do not be tempted to add to it. Fire is a major hazard in countryside that is always parched during the summer months (and sometimes all year round after a drought). Respect this country code and ensure that this beautiful area remains unspoiled.

- **Take all your litter away with you.**
- **Do not light fires or throw away cigarette ends.**
- **Protect all wild and cultivated plants.** Don't pick wild flowers. Never cross cultivated land, and do not be tempted to pick cherries, citrus fruits, almonds or olives — these are clearly someone's private property.
- **Do not disturb or frighten animals or birds.**
- **Protect water sources.** *Fonts* (springs) in the mountains are especially important. When attending to 'calls of nature' keep well away from springs and streams, and make sure that you bury all paper.
- **Walkers — do not take risks!** Never walk alone and always tell someone where you are going and when you expect to return. It might be helpful also to leave this information on a note in your hotel room. Remember that any route could become dangerous after storms or bulldozing. If you are lost or injured you may have to wait a long time for help. *Deep gorges* should always be treated with care and caution. Walkers have disappeared or died in the mountains of the Costa Blanca. Usually the cause of these accidents is carelessness and lack of common sense.

2b XABIA'S *MOLINOS* (map page 48, photograph page 50)

🚗 car or taxi to the Santuario de Nuestra Señora de los Angeles on the Cap de Sant Antoni road (Car tour 1); 21min on foot from the Santuario, or 12min if you drive up to the crest (limited parking). Walk up Camí del Monastir, then follow Walk 2b from the 25min-point (page 48). No shade, but rocky plinths to sit on and fantastic views across Xábia Bay.

2c CREU DEL PORTITXOL (map page 49, photograph page 11)

🚗 by car or taxi from Xábia (Car tour 1); 4min or 21min on foot. Follow Walk 2c (page 49) for 4min, to picnic on the grassy terraces or at the cliff edge. Shade of pines if you want it, magnificent views, lovely ambience. Or follow Walk 2c for about 10min, then take the eroded path on the left which leads to steps down to Cala Sardinera (21min), a secluded pebbly beach, with clear water for a swim. No shade.

2d CALPE CALAS (map page 49)

🚗 by car or 🚌 bus to Cala Calalga (30km point on Car tour 1); up to 54min on foot. Follow Walk 2d (page 50). Every cove is a possible picnic spot, but we particularly recommend the one at the end of the walk. It's secluded, there are flat rocks to sit on, and the location and views are fantastic. No shade.

3 ERMITA VELLA (map page 52)

🚗 by car to Calpe station (Car tour 1), then drive to the alternative starting point for Walk 3 (see page 51). Follow the walk to the 33min-point; 20min on foot. There are well laid out picnic benches, toilets, an 'old' (2003 vintage!) *ermita* and great views.

5 PUNTA DE LA ESCALETA, SERRA GELADA (map page 57)

🚗 by car, taxi or on foot to Benidorm's Playa Levante (Car tour 1). You can either drive to within 200m of the picnic spot, or follow coastal paths for 40min. Follow Short walk 5-2 (page 56). This rocky promontory offers no shade, but there are magnificent views round the coast to Benidorm. You could also follow a path up to the 17th-century *torre*, to look out to the cliffs of the Serra Gelada.

Picnic 10b: The lavadero *at Flecix*

6a, b SERPIS RIVER (map pages 60-61)

🚗 to L'Orxa station (Car tour 2); either 12min or 46min on foot. (a) Follow Walk 6 (page 59) for 9min, then take the track to the right. In a few minutes you will come to abandoned grassy terraces on the left, a pleasant spot overlooking the river, with shade from old olive trees. (b) Follow the walk to the 46min-point, then turn right to the low dam. Sit on the dam wall, listen to the sound of running water and watch the fish swimming. There is some shade nearby.

8a, b THE ENCHANTED POOLS (map page 67)

🚗 to the 29km marker, about 2km east of Planes, on the CV700 (Car tour 2); 16min or 31min on foot. (a) Follow Walk 8 (page 65) as far as the pools (16min 🏕). Refresh yourself with the cool water or just sit on the steps. There is a *font* nearby and shade from the sides of the gorge. (b) For a more natural spot, continue as far as the small reservoir (31min). Shade, running water, rocks to sit on and 'English meadow' atmosphere.

10a THE EBO RIVER (map pages 70-71)

🚗 to Vall d'Ebo (the 33km point on Car tour 2); 20min on foot (or only 11min, if you drive to the cemetery). Follow Walk 10 from the 3h33min- point (page 76). Choose your spot by the river, at its best when flowing. Little shade but flat rocks, deep pools and the beautiful sound of running water. Alternatively continue up to Font Xili. Shade, stone seats, views over valley and hills and fresh, clear water from the *font*.

10b-d VALL DE LAGUAR (map pages 70-71, photographs opposite and pages 72-73)

🚗 to Fleix (Car tour 1); 5-45min on foot. Follow Alternative walk 10 (page 73). (b) Picnic at the *lavadero* shown opposite (5min; stone seats, font, shade) or, for more spectacular settings, also with shade: (c) descend steeply down the Mozarabic trail shown on pages 72-73, to the cave and waterfall (30min); (d) go all the way down to the floor of the Río Ebo (45min).

11a, b FINCA BIXAUCA and CASA TANCAT (map page 78)

🚗 to the CV752 near Tárbena (Car tours 1 and 3); 3min or 25min on foot. Follow Walk 11 (page 77). (a) At 3min the grassy area beside Finca Bixauca has terrace walls to sit on, shade if you want it and fantastic views. If you venture into the longer grass in the summer be aware of the possibility of snakes. (b) At the 9min-point, fork left and descend steeply into the valley, where an old house, surrounded by cherry trees, is an idyllic and secluded setting overlooked by rugged peaks and the high cliffs of Paso Tancat. (This is the 2h53min-point on the main walk.)

12 FONTS DE L'ALGAR (map page 81, photograph page 23)

🚗 to Fonts de l'Algar (Car tour 1); no walking. Follow 'How to get there' at the top of Walk 12 (page 80), to park at Casa Federico. On weekdays out of season it is very quiet here, and you can sit at the side of the pools, by the little waterfalls (no shade).

13a, b FONT MOLI (map page 86) 🏕

🚗 to Guadalest (Car tour 3); no walking, or 10min on foot. Follow 'How to get there' at the top of Walk 13 (page 85), to park at Font Molí. (a) Here there is a *font* and picnic benches on two levels — but little shade. (b) For a more inspiring spot make a start on Walk 13 and at the 6min-point take the track straight ahead, to a flat shaded area (10min). There are two rickety picnic tables, or take a blanket and sit on the ground overlooking the valley and the mountains to the north.

16 FONT DE PARTEGAT (map page 93)

🚐 to Font de Partegat (Car tour 3); no walking. This *Area Recreativa*, on the route of Walks 13 and 16, is in a fantastic setting, surrounded by massive cliffs and rocky outcrops. There's a font, stone benches, barbecue facilities and shade. Plenty of opportunity for strolling. Avoid weekends and *fiestas*, when it is very busy.

18a BARRANC DEL SINC (map pages 100-101, photograph page 103)

🚐 to Alcoi (Car tour 4); 8min on foot. Follow 'How to get there' at the top of Walk 18 to park near the brickworks. Then follow the walk for 8min. Delightful area beside the cobbled path and steps which lead up the *barranco*. There are rocks to sit on, and the towering cliffs provide plenty of shade. After heavy rains there will be water in the *barranco*.

18b, c SANT CRISTOFOL (map pages 100-101) 🏞

🚐 to Cocentaina (Car tour 4); no walking, or 25min on foot. (b) At the roundabout, just before leaving the town, turn left to Sant Cristófol, and drive up to this *zona recreativa* (about 1km). The large terraced complex has an attractive picnic and barbecue area as well as a *font*, some caves, a *mirador*, a bar-restaurant and plenty of shade. (c) Drive *past* the picnic site and continue up the concrete road to a *mirador* just below Cocentaina castle. A path leads to the castle in about 10min, but for the picnic spot turn sharp right at the *mirador* and follow Alternative walk 18 (but in reverse) for 25min — to an idyllic setting under the cliff, on the top terrace of almond and olive groves. There is shade, rocks and planks to sit on and magnificent views over to Serrella and Aitana.

19 ERMITA DE LA MARE DE DEU (map pages 100-101) 🏞

🚐 to Agres (Car tour 4) and follow signs to the *ermita* and convent; no walking. There is a bar-restaurant here, but the nearby picnic benches are in a beautiful setting, with views over the Agres valley. Shade, *font*.

20 FONT MARIOLA (map pages 100-101) 🏞

🚐 to Font Mariola (Car tour 4); no walking. See Car tour 4 at the 100km-point (page 32), to drive to the *font*. It could be busy here in season and at weekends, but otherwise this is an idyllic spot. There are benches, ample shade, a large water tank and a little *canaleta* running by.

21 FONT ROJA (map page 114, photograph page 113) 🏞

🚐 to the Parque Natural de Font Roja (optional detour at the 55km-point on Car tour 4); no walking. Extensive picnic areas in the pines, with benches, barbecue areas, water. Heavily wooded, with several signposted walks. Avoid on Sundays or in high season.

22 PENAGUILA CASTLE VIEW (map page 116)

🚐 to El Coyao on the A171 about 3km before Penáguila (Car tour 4); 10min on foot. Follow Walk 22 from the 24min-point (page 117) as far as the crest. This rocky vantage point is in full sun, but views of the castle and surrounding mountains and valleys are breathtaking.

The 'forgotten finca' (Picnic 25a) is worth exploring — it has a functioning well, an old canaleta, and (about 50m/yds behind the house) a large underground tunnel.

23a POU DEL SURDO (map page 121, photograph page 119)

🚐 or 🚌 (Car tour 4) to Port de la Carrasqueta; 23min on foot. Follow Walk 23 (page 119) as far as the *pou*. There is plenty to explore, an old snow well, some shade if you want it, and fine views.

23b MAS DE LA COVA (map page 121)

🚌 to La Sarga (Car tour 4); no walking necessary but, for the agile, there is an optional climb up to some prehistoric cave paintings. Park at Mas de la Cova (see the 136km-point on page 34). The house is uninhabited, but its fields still cultivated. A peaceful spot, some shady trees and places to sit. On the hillside, overhanging rocks shelter caves containing prehistoric paintings, and the path to them can be seen clearly from here. It is steep and narrow and it will take about 10min to negotiate.

24 RAMBLA DELS MOLINS (map on reverse of touring map)

🚌 to the Catí-Petrer road (see Car tour 5 after 93km; page 38); up to 20min on foot. Follow Walk 24 (page 122) from the 3h14min-point, from the restaurant down into the river bed. A particularly spectacular setting under steep sandy cliffs is reached after about 16min. Oleanders grow along the river bed, there are rocks to sit on and shade if required.

25a FORGOTTEN *FINCA* (map on reverse of touring map, photograph above)

🚌 to Castalla (Car tour 5); 50min on foot (or 35min if you drive as far as Fam, Fum y Fret). See 'How to get there' at the top of Walk 25 (page 126), then follow the Short walk to the *finca* shown below. A secluded spot overlooking the Castalla valley, with shade and plenty to explore.

25b ERMITA DE CATI (map on reverse of touring map)

🚌 to Xorret de Catí (Car tour 5 after 86km); 20min on foot. From the hotel head south on the road (walkers' signpost PR-V29). After 2min turn left uphill on a track. Pass the large Casa de la Administración on your right, with a nearby *nevera* (9min). At a junction of tracks (15min) go right; this leads to the *ermita*. Fabulous far-reaching views over El Cid and the Serra de Maigmó. Shade in surrounding pine woods.

✸Touring

Our five car tours cover the northern and central parts of Alicante Province. Each tour begins from one of the major tourist towns on the coast; wherever you are based, the starting point is easily accessible.

There are **three main types of road** in this part of the country. The AP7 *autopista*, or motorway, which runs north to south is the quickest way to travel between coastal towns. However, it is a toll road and quite expensive. The parallel N332 tends to become congested even outside the tourist season and progress can be slow. Some of our tours follow parts of the A31 *autovia*, the main inland road north from Alicante, and it presents few traffic problems. Other roads tend to be narrow and, in the mountains, rather winding. They carry relatively little traffic, but what traffic there is might well be travelling in the middle of the road ... and going either very fast or very slowly. *Take great care at all times and expect the unexpected.* There is a great deal of road construction and upgrading going on in the area, and road numbers do change. We have tried to give sufficient instructions to ensure that this causes only minor irritation.

Many of the towns or villages on the tours are well worth exploring, whether to visit their museums, study their architecture or just to absorb their atmosphere. We recommend that you **park somewhere suitable and continue on foot**, particularly through the older quarters. Streets were built to accommodate pedestrians or donkey carts, not motor vehicles; even in the smallest of cars you may find yourself in a very 'tight spot'.

Our touring notes are brief, giving only the minimum of historical detail. Instead we place emphasis on times and distances, road conditions and possibilities for sightseeing, **picnicking** and **walking**. During a long car tour you may encounter a landscape which you would like to explore at leisure another day.

Our touring times allow for no stops or detours

Outside Altea la Vella, Campana, Ponoch and Aitana rise above almond groves (Car tour 3).

16

and, of course, assume driving within the speed limit. **The pull-out touring map is designed to be held out opposite the touring notes**; **symbols** on the map correspond to those in the text. On main roads you will find that **petrol stations** are plentiful; in the mountains some of the small villages have a pump (well signposted and open during normal business hours).

When touring *do* make sure that you always carry **plenty of water**. A car can become very hot and uncomfortable in the sunshine, and there is not always a convenient bar just where you might want one. If you intend stopping en route to buy **food**, remember to do so before shops close up for their extended lunch break. All the towns and most of the villages you will pass through have bars. Those that don't provide full meals usually have a selection of *tapas* or can make up a *bocadillo*. Bars and petrol stations are likely to have toilets and telephone.

In winter it can be cold and windy in the mountains so take adequate **warm clothing**. Whatever the time of year, **the sun can be strong**. Suncream and head covering are a must if you wander in the villages, stop for a picnic or take a stroll. Even with our long experience of Spain, we are sometimes surprised at the strength of the sun.

Allow plenty of time for the tours. You will derive little pleasure from rushing from place to place. The pace of life, especially in rural Spain, is slow, and you will do well to imitate it. Stop and explore or investigate things that catch your eye. We have found that it is often purely by chance that we stumble on something quite delightful.

Please heed the country code on page 11.

1 COSTA BLANCA NEW AND OLD

Benidorm • Cap de la Nau • Xábia • Cap de Sant Antoni • Dénia • Orba • Fleix • Fonts de l'Algar • Benidorm

179km/111mi; 4-5 hours' driving; exit C from Benidorm (plan page 8)

On route: 🎡 at Penyal d'Ifach, Cap de Sant Antoni, Cova de les Calaveres, Fonts de l'Algar, Polop, La Nucia; Picnics (see **P** symbol and pages 10-15): 2b-d, 3, 5, 10b-d, 11, 12; Walks 1-3, 5, 10, 11, 12

If you have time for only one car tour this is the one to do. The heavily-populated, affluent coastal strip is picturesque and fascinating, contrasting starkly with the landscape presented as you turn in towards the mountains. Then you are suddenly confronted with vast open spaces, layer upon layer of serras, tiny villages clinging to hillsides and picture-postcard views of mountain peaks. This is the real Costa Blanca, and we hope that it whets your appetite for exploring on foot.

Leave Benidorm from Rincón de l'Oix, at the eastern end of Playa Levante: take the northbound Avinguda de Ametlla de Mar. (To the right at this junction is the road to **P**5 and the start of Walk 5). After 3km turn right for Platja de l'Albir. The road runs through orange groves, parallel to the Serra Gelada — its ridge looking quite benign from this side. Turn right for Platja de l'Albir again (7km); after about 0.5km you pass the road where Walk 5 brings you from the Serra Gelada into **l'Albir** (8km ✗). Continue through the town on the main road, close to the shore, following signs for Altea. The Albir lighthouse stands out prominently at the end of the serra, while ahead, behind Altea church, is the flattish-topped mountain of Oltá, focus of Walk 3.

In **Altea** (10km ✝ ▲▲ ✗ 🖳) drive past the yacht and fishing harbours, and take the road along the seafront. Then turn left up to the parallel main road (N332) whenever you wish (it may depend on traffic). Pass palm-fringed villas hidden behind walls dripping with bougainvilleas and cross the estuary of the Algar and Guadalest rivers, before reaching a crest. Below are the moorings of a private yacht club and, ahead, the remains of Calpe Castle high on a peak at the end of the Serra de Toix.

Immediately after passing through the Mascarat tunnels a closer view of Oltá presents itself ahead and soon afterwards Penyal d'Ifach comes into sight. At 22km take the turn-off right for Calpe Sur. (Just beyond the turn, a road goes up left to the railway station, starting point for Walk 3.) Enter **Calpe** (24km ⛁ ✝ ▲▲ ✗ 🖳⊕) and follow the main road downhill, heading towards Penyal d'Ifach. Apart from this amazing rock (see opposite) and a couple of good beaches, Calpe also has its own *salinas* — salt pools — which are just to the left of the road (25km). You will notice flamingos as you drive by, but a short stroll will also reveal many waders. At the end of the *salinas* turn right and follow signs to Penyal d'Ifach. Park where you can, just before the information boards (it could be very busy here in the summer). Leave your car for a while and admire the views of the Serra Gelada and Calpe Bay (🚏💺) — perhaps taking a short walk in these beautiful surroundings.

Return to the *salinas* and turn right towards Playa Levante, parallel with the sea. Oltá rises on your left. After the Hotel Esmeralda, note a road on the right to Cala Calalga. Walk 2d (*P*2d) starts 300m down this road. Stop at the *mirador* (31km 📷) for views of Cap de Moraira, Penyal d'Ifach and the coast. Pass the beach resorts of Benissa, itself situated a few kilometres inland. After cresting a rise, you return to sea level, passing promenade gardens. At the first roundabout in **Moraira** (40km ✘🛍), turn left on the CV743 following signs for Teulada and curling above healthy vineyards. At a fork (42km) go right for Benitatxell and Xábia, noticing the antennas crowning the Cumbre del Sol on the right, before climbing to enter **Benitatxell** (46km).

Turn right on the CV740 for Xábia. Pass a football ground and go right again (47km) on a road signposted to Camí Cansalaes. On the descent, vineyards gradually give way to almond trees. Pass El Campo (✘) and The Inn on the Green. Follow the road as it sweeps round past some villas and the Restaurante Carrasco on the right (51km), and go right on the main Cap de la Nau road (CV742). Continue through woods and between vines and almond trees until you come to a right-hand bend

Penyal d'Ifach rises 360m/1200ft above the Salinas de Calpe. Taken from Oltá (Walk 3)

where, straight ahead, a cross — the Creu del Portitxol — overlooks the coast. This viewpoint (55km ☞) is the starting point for **P**2c and Walk 2c to Cap Prim (in summer, parking could be difficult). Continue winding up the hill where yet more development threatens to spoil this heavily-wooded area. Pass a turn off right to Granadella (57km), a secluded cove. The road becomes more built-up and descends to the lighthouse of **Cap de la Nau★** (59km ✕☞). There are superb coastal views from the *mirador*.

Turn round and go back towards Xábia. Views are quite different from this new perspective. The rocky mass of Montgó (photograph page 11) immediately dominates the skyline ahead, becoming ever more impressive as you draw nearer. Ignore a left turn to Benitatxell (67km) and continue towards **Xábia** (♣▲▲✕➡⊕M; Walk 2a). At the end of the dual carriageway, pass McDonald's and Lidl, then turn left to pass the Día supermarket (71km). At the roundabout bear right uphill. Follow the one-way system always uphill, then turn right for Dénia and Cap de Sant Antoni. This is the Carretera de Dénia (CV736) which zigzags up and out of Xábia. Just after you leave the town boundary you will see the Ermita de Santa Lucia (♣) atop a hill to your left and, a little further on, an entrance to the Parque Natural del Montgó. Soon afterwards, turn right (74km) for Cap de Sant Antoni. The road takes you through pleasant wooded countryside, past villas and haciendas and, on the right, the imposing Santuario de Nuestra Señora de los Angeles (♣; parking for **P**2b). A couple of kilometres further on, Walk 2b starts at the *zona recreativa* on the left (☰). The road then crests the hill, opening up views of Cap de Sant Antoni lighthouse and over the coast to Cap de la Nau and Xábia Bay. From the *mirador* just before **Cap de Sant Antoni★** lighthouse (78km ☞) admire the majestic cliffs of the headland visited in Walk 2a.

Return to the Dénia road, turn right and drive around the base of Montgó. Just past the Campo de Tiro (shooting range; 82km), the road reaches a crest from where, on a clear day, you can see all the way to Valencia and beyond, with Dénia in the foreground. At this point there is another entrance to the Parque Natural.

From here the road winds down into **Dénia** (⌂♣▲▲ Δ ✕➡⊕M; see plan on page 9). Go straight on at the round-about and through the outer suburbs to the promenade (87km). The road continues past the harbour to the large

'Cruz Roja' roundabout. You want to go left here, so take the last exit along Ferrándiz Patricio. Note the railway station off to the left, follow the traffic flow to the left and then take the first right into Passeig de Saladar, a wide road mostly taken up by a palm-lined central reservation and many parked cars. Turn left at the second crossroads (Carrer de Diana, just after Bar Noelia), cross the railway and go straight ahead up Camí de Sant Joan, heading for Montgó. Fork right at the Al Khalif mosque, then turn right into Assagador de Santa Llúcia (92km). At an open area take the left fork signed to Pare Pere (93km). This quite pretty and ornate Franciscan *ermita* is still in use and is a popular place for visitors.

Continue past the *ermita* as the road winds downhill. It becomes Carretera de la Colonia. Straightaway you will pass, on the left, the Dénia entrance to the Parque Natural del Montgó. Walk 1 starts here. The road winds down to a junction where you turn left into Assagador de Cabanes (later Pou de la Muntanya); this takes you through a housing estate, with views of Dénia castle ahead. Cross the railway line back into Dénia and go straight on at the next junction. At the MAPFRE roundabout, take the exit past the MAPFRE building signposted to San Carlos hospital. Keep on this road, following the Alicante signs, past the Campsa station (🚘), and go straight on at the next four roundabouts. You have now left Dénia and should take the well-signposted slip road into **La Xara** (99km). Pedreguer, your next destination, is signposted straight ahead.

Drive through **La Xara**, heading for the hills and away from the tourist beat. Now you can relax a little and enjoy the gentle rural countryside, old villages perched on hillsides and some spectacular mountains. Pass through groves of oranges and date palms before reaching a set of traffic lights. Go straight across and into **Pedreguer** (105km). Follow signs to Benidoleig on the CV733 taking care not to miss a sharp right turn. As you drive through a fertile valley, the old sturdy *fincas* make a change from white villas, and the serras ahead give you a taste of what is to come. Rounding a bend just after some picnic benches (110km 🍴), come to the **Cova de les Calaveres★**, where prehistoric remains are to be seen along with stalactites, stalagmites and rock domes over 20m/ 65ft high.

In **Benidoleig** (111km) keep straight on towards Orba. Ahead is the Vall de Laguar and rising to the left the serra shown on page 1, Cavall Verd (Green Horse). Depending on which account you read, the ridge was named for its physical appearance or after a Moorish knight who used to appear there on a green horse to defend his territory. At **Orba** (115km ⌂♣✕) follow signs for Fontilles (at one T-junction the sign is cunningly placed behind you on the left). Wind up through olive groves and citrus orchards, with magnificent views (📷) of the surrounding serras and valleys. At a junction (118km), take the left fork signposted to Fontilles. Notice the defile created by the Ebo River, clearly visible in the valley to the right. You soon pass the road to the Sanatorio de Fontilles, a leper colony dating from 1909. It is also a research centre. The road ascends, with stunning panoramas (📷), into the Vall de Laguar, through **Campell** and up to **Fleix** (122km). Continue up the road. If you have waited till now to picnic, park at the school — the starting point for Walk 10. A few metres up the road, where it continues to Benimaurell, take the track off right. You can picnic at the *lavadero* shown on page 12 or follow the Mozarabic trail shown on pages 72-73 down to a cave, a waterfall and the valley floor (**P**10b-d).

Return through Fleix and Campell, gaining intermittent views of Orba castle perched prominently on top of a crag. At the entrance to Orba (128km), turn right for Benidorm (CV715; 129km ⛽). Contour around the slopes, then zigzag uphill. You will get closer views of Orba castle from here with the impressive peaks of Cavall Verd to its left. The road then descends through olive groves, crosses the Jalón River and climbs again. Just after the 15km marker, notice the isolated building, with a pine tree in front, set up on the saddle ahead to the left — the restaurant on the Coll de Rates. At **Parcent** (133km ♣✕) the road heads right towards Tárbena and winds steeply uphill. *Miradors* (📷 138km; 140.5km) give fantastic views over the valley.

From the Coll de Rates (540m/1770ft; 141km ✕) the road descends above the Barranc de Binarreal in what locals call the Tárbena Valley. It is surrounded by astonishing serras, and on a clear day the views are breathtaking. You might see choughs playing around the rocky slopes and cavorting over the valley as the road undulates through terraced hillsides, giving a fresh view at every turn. Pass the CV752 off right (148km) to the start of Walk 11 (and **P**11) and continue into **Tárbena** (149km ✕). Then wind down to another *mirador* (152km 📷), from where you can see the amazing Bolulla Castle stuck on its crag (⌂) — and also down to Benidorm. Alternative walk 12-2 starts and ends at this viewpoint.

Continue to descend steeply, passing sheer crags and deep gorges, the most impressive being the Paso Tancat, to **Bolulla** (156km). As you leave the village, Penya Severino, the culmination of the Bernia Ridge, dominates the view to the left and does so all the way down to the Algar Valley. Blessed with a great deal of underground water, this valley is one of the most fertile in the area.

Turn left (159km) on the road sign-posted to **Fonts de l'Algar★** (✕ 吊 △**M**) and, 1km downhill, look for the restaurant Casa Federico on the left: out of season you will be able to use its car park, which is just along-side some attractive pools (**P**12). Walk 12 starts here. In high season, continue up through the development to the main car park at the top of the hill. The complex, with waterfalls (shown here), *fonts* and other attractions, is worth ex-ploring.

Fonts de l'Algar

Return to the main road and continue into **Callosa d'En Sarriá** (165km ╬ ▲▲ ✕ 🖃 ⊕M). At the roundabout in the centre go left (signposted to Benidorm). Cross the Gua-dalest River (167km) and soon Campana comes into view, towering ahead of you. Drive through **Polop** (169km), past gardens (吊) on the right. You might like to stop briefly in Polop to look at its fountain which has 221 spouts (yes, really) and is decorated in tiles representing the shields of all the administrative areas of Alicante. Continue along a crescent-shaped 'esplanade' road, lined with a lighted walkway with blue walls, into **La Nucia** (170km). Leaving La Nucia (吊), the Serra Gelada again looms into view. Pass a road off right to Finestrat (177km) and follow the road all the way back into Benidorm (179km), then use the plan (page 8) to find the best route back to your hotel.

Dénia • Pego • Planes de la Baronía • Beniarrés • L'Orxa • Vall de Gallinera • L'Atzubia • Dénia

120km/74mi; just over 3 hours' driving; exit A from Dénia (plan page 9)

On route: ⋒ at the limekilns, Alcalá, L'Orxa; Picnics (see **P** symbol and pages 10-15): 6, 8, 10a; Walks 6-9

This tour is probably the most scenic in the area. It follows the northern valleys where every available plot of land is cultivated. While orange, almond and olive trees abound, the abundant cherry trees leave the most lasting impression. The area is particularly attractive after spring rains, when it is lusciously green, and the trees are in full blossom. You will have spectacular views of surrounding serras, including the unusual horned peaks of the Serra de Benicadell. Enjoy them, but take care on the many bends in the narrow valley roads. Some motorists may find the sheer drops on several stretches unnerving. Once you enter the mountains, Planes is the only place where petrol is available.

L eave Dénia by Exit A (signposted 'Autovía', 'Alicante'), meeting the main Alicante-Valencia N332 road after 9km, in Ondara. Turn right towards Valencia. *Carefully* keep to the N332 until you can take the signposted exit for the CV700. When you meet the CV700, turn *sharp right* for Pego, heading back the way you came and eventually passing under the motorway. Pego is directly ahead, nestling at the foot of the mountains, its church prominent against the hillside. It is an important town and might well be called the 'gateway to the mountains'. Shortly after entering **Pego** (20km ⬜✝🏔✕🅿⊕) turn left at the roundabout and zigzag through the outskirts following signs for Sagra and Callosa. Watch for the 1km marker and, just beyond it (21km) turn right on the CV712 for Vall d'Ebo, winding steeply up a narrow road through pine woods. After about 5km there are magnificent views (📷) over Pego deep in the valley, overlooked by its castle high on a hill. You are right in the heart of the mountains, enjoying spectacular scenery.

After rounding the hillsides, the road climbs to a pass (29km), with an old converted windmill on the right. Just over the crest a deep gorge, the Barranc del Infern, cuts through the barren mountains (📷). Descend through market gardens and orchards. On the approach to Vall d'Ebo you cross a blue-painted bridge (33km). About 30m straight ahead there is a road to the left where you could park, to take a stroll along the river (**P**10a). But the tour turns right and bypasses Vall d'Ebo (✝✕⊕△), following the river.

Turn right across another bridge and drive out of the valley, past a huge cave, the Cova del Rull★ (⋒ 36km).

Soon the natural rock arch at the end of the Serra de Foradá comes into sight ahead. Then, in a sheltered spot just before another bridge, you encounter the first of the many cherry orchards. Cross the high plateau, the road lined in places with sage, rosemary and thyme (sorry, no parsley!) and the air alive with flocks of goldfinch. Make a stop at 43km to visit the ancient limekilns (⋒) and a *nevera* (snow well), then continue past **Alcalá de la Jovada** (44km ⋒△). Both Vall d'Ebo and Alcalá have vastly reduced populations now, but originally formed an important part of the territory of the legendary Moorish ruler known as Al Azraq. This cherry route was all part of his 13th-century 'kingdom', and many of the terraced lands you see owe their structure to the Moors he ruled.

Pass by the village of **Margarida** (⬚✗), then turn left (50km) on the Vall de Gallinera road (CV700), passing the Venta de Margarida. Just after crossing the Pont de les Calderes (53km), opposite the 29km marker, a narrow road leads to the Barranco de la Encantada (Walk 8). Why not park on the left about 100m past the bridge and take a walk along the *barranco* (*P*8)? Continue to **Planes de la Baronía** (⬚♣✗☕△), overlooked by the Ermita de Santo Cristo. Planes is worth a detour for petrol and to see its setting around the medieval castle and old aqueduct which still serves the wash-house.

But the main tour bypasses Planes: just at the petrol sign, turn right for Beniarrés (54km). This little road descends steeply into the valley. As you climb out the other side, notice steps on the right to the *ermita* (♣) high above. On the left catch sight of a reservoir, the Embalse de Beniarrés, and the village's little white church standing prominently on top of a hill, with Benicadell rising majestically behind it (photograph page 66). The road descends to the *embalse,* where we have seen osprey, herons, cormorants, ducks and other waterbirds. Cross the dam (60km) and continue round the other side to **Beniarrés** (64km ♣). When you reach the junction with the CV701 turn right and drive past the village following the wide valley of the river Serpis towards L'Orxa (Lorcha). The valley, heavily wooded and cultivated (more cherries), is green throughout the year and the high mountain ahead of you is Safor, climbed in Walk 7.

Just as you approach a bridge over the river Serpis, a road on your left leads 0.5km uphill to the old railway station shown on page 63, starting point for Walk 6 through the Serpis Valley. Cross the bridge and turn right

PERPUTXENT CASTLE
This impressive fortress, setting for Picnic 6, was initially the stronghold of Al Azraq before being reconquered by Jaime I. It subsequently came into the hands of the Knights Templar, was confiscated and came under the power of Jaime II. It then passed to the new Orden Militar de Santa María de Montesa.

(71km) into **L'Orxa** (72km ☐🍴), at the end of the Serpis Gorge and protected by the Castell de Perputxent (**P**6; photograph left). Walk 7 starts at Font Grota (🍴), at the entrance to the village, in a garden on your right. Drive past the village, alongside the dry river bed. Just where the road looks as if it is running out, turn left, away from the village. You wind steeply up to the ridge behind L'Orxa on a narrow but well-surfaced road, with fine views of Benicadell off to the right (photograph page 4). Drive past terraces all the way to the top, then head across the flat-topped ridge to a junction and a STOP sign (78km). Turn right, and descend towards the Serra de Foradá.

Very tight hairpin bends take you into the **Vall de Gallinera**. Cross a (usually dry) ford and turn left to **Alpatró** (82km). Here rejoin the CV700, turning left towards Pego. Almond and orange orchards grace the terraces, but soon it becomes evident that each little village along this route derives its living from the abundant cherry trees. In the spring you'll be surrounded by the beauty and fragrance of the blossom; in summer you can stop and buy the fruit. The road runs high above the *barranco* and there are some fantastic views down the Gallinera Valley (83km 📷). You pass through the little settlements of **La Carroja** (🍴), **Benissivá** and **Benialí**. The turret of Gallinera Castle (Walk 9, photograph page 69) comes into view on top of a hill ahead, and steep cliffs close in on either side as you leave the valley.

The countryside eventually opens out again into terraced orchards surrounding **L'Atzubia** (97km), where Walk 9 begins, and Pego comes into view straight ahead. From **Pego** (101km), follow signs for Dénia, bypassing the centre and retracing your outgoing route back to Dénia (120km).

3 CENTRAL VALLEYS — THE ALMOND ROUTE

Calpe • Callosa d'En Sarriá • Guadalest • Confrides • Gorga • Castell de Castells • Xaló/Jalón • Calpe

135km/84mi; 3-4 hours' driving from Calpe

On route: 🍴 at Callosa, Confrides, Quatretondeta, Castell de Castells; Picnics (see **P** symbol and pages 10-15): 11, 13, 15, 16; Walks 3, 11, 13, 15, 16

Mountains surround you on the outward route through the picturesque Guadalest Valley and on the return along a narrow, winding road through the Jalón Valley. Almond groves are a major feature of the landscape: in January and February large areas are ablaze with pink and white blossom. But at any time, the variety of scenery provided by the two valleys with their surrounding serras makes this tour unforgettable.

Leave Calpe (Walk 3) from the Plaza Central. Drive up the hill following signs to Alicante and join the N332 going south. Every bit of land has been developed for housing. Calpe Castle is prominent as you continue under the railway line, down into the Mascarat Gorge and through three tunnels cut from the sheer rock of the mountainside. Take the right fork signposted to Callosa d'En Sarriá (9km), then turn right again for Callosa and go under the A7 motorway, past a petrol station (10km 🚬).

You are now on the CV755 and almost immediately going through **Altea la Vella**, an upmarket residential area situated just under the Bernia Ridge. Take in the amazing views shown on pages 16-17, of Campana, Ponoch and the Serra de Aitana, ahead and to the left, as you drive through seemingly endless citrus groves. In stark contrast to the barren mountains, the countryside stretching out at either side of the road is lush and green. As well as the more common fruit and nut trees there are large groves of *nísperos* (medlars), easily distinguished by their much denser and darker foliage.

At the roundabout in the centre of **Callosa d'En Sarriá** (19km ✝🏔✗🚬⊕M) take the exit to Alcoi and Guadalest. The road (🍴) skirts high above the Guadalest with fantastic views encompassing the valley and Guadalest Castle. Just before crossing the river (✗ and **M** of old motorcycles) the serras of Aixorta and Serrella dominate the landscape as the road winds quite steeply uphill. On rounding the bend, just after a bar with a commanding view of the valley, enjoy your first close-up of the remains of Guadalest Castle perched on top of its rocky outcrop. Further round, houses come into view, clinging precariously to the slopes below the castle. As you pass a rather grand drystone wall and a *mirador*

27

(28km 📷), the buttresses of Penya Mulero (Walk 13), much favoured by golden eagles, rise on the left.

Pass a road off to the right (30km) to the Embalse de Guadalest; it leads to the start of Walk 15. **Guadalest★** (31km 🅿✕M📷) is a one-street village of scarcely 200 inhabitants. But in summer it is bristling with tourists on account of its superb setting. The rocks rise up alongside the road and the *mirador* (📷) at the castle affords a magnificent panorama of the surrounding serras. As you drive through the village you enjoy a first view of Benifató Castle in the distance. At a roundabout go straight on (CV70 to Alcoi), immediately passing a turn-off left to El Trestellador restaurant (33km); Walk 13 starts about 1.5km up this road (*P*13).

Pass through **Benimantell** (✕) and climb up past Restaurante Venta Benifató to a junction (36km). Turn left and, about 500m further on, at the village sign for **Benifató** (🅿), turn sharp right for 'Font de Partegat' (the sign may be partially hidden by some rubbish bins). This narrow and winding road heads up towards the buttresses of Partegat. Pass the little road where Walk 16 comes in from the right and reach **Font de Partegat** (40km; *P*16). Walk 16 heads upwards from here but, for the car tour, return the same way after you have explored a bit. Then turn left at the main road to **Confrides** (49km ✝▲✕). From here the road climbs past El Basquet, selling local cheeses, preserves, etc, and through a pass (966m; 53km ✕📷), before descending into the next valley. The hills ahead, being less rocky, are more gentle, and there are many paths ribboning up the slopes which are wooded or terraced almost to the tops.

Continue through **Benasau** (60km ✝✕). Cocentaina Castle (🅿) stands out on the stark hillside ahead just before you turn right on the CV710 (63km) for Gorga. This road undulates through pretty rural countryside to **Gorga** (67km), where it takes a sharp right turn (CV754) towards Quatretondeta. You are now heading eastwards again on the northern side of the Serra de Serrella; the soft rock makes for some unusual formations. Drive across several bridges which span a series of shallow gorges before winding up past **Quatretondeta** (72km ▲✕🍴).

As the narrow road contours round the slopes watch for small birds. Some will only be summer visitors, but the chirpy serins with their yellow flashes abound in the fruit trees all year. When you join the CV720 at **Facheca**, a little village tucked into the hillside (77km), turn right and pass the old village of **Famorca** (80km). The road, now wider but still winding, crosses more dry river beds. The spectacular Serra de Aixorta becomes visible ahead, with Serrella Castle on a peak to its right (85km ⌨). Wind gradually downhill towards picturesque **Castell de Castells** (88km ♣ ▲ ✕), nestling in the valley below. Just before entering the village, turn right at the bridge (☰) towards Tárbena. Park by the picnic tables, if you wish to explore Castell de Castells, a maze of narrow streets.

Then continue along the winding CV752. Just past the 3km road marker (97km) a road to the right marks the start of Walk 11 (*P*11). The long ridge of Ferrer and the rugged peaks of Bernia rise on the left. On the outskirts of **Tárbena** (100km ✕) turn left on the CV715. The road affords views into the Binarreal Valley (Walk 12) as it contours to the Coll de Rates (540m/1770ft; 107km ✕). Wind down into the Jalón Valley, past two viewpoints (⌨ 107.5km, 110km), towards **Parcent** (114km ♣✕). Just before this village, which is dominated by its church, turn right on the A142 for Alcalalí. Almond groves lead the eye to the Serra del Cavall Verd (photograph page 1). Just after entering **Alcalalí** (117km ✕) turn right on the CV720 (a sign indicates ☎ 3km away).

Xaló/Jalón★ (120km ♣ ▲ ✕☎) is very much given over to expatriates and tourists. Many of the streets (and the dry river bed) are lined with flea-market stalls on Saturdays; restaurants and *bodegas* abound. As the road bears right, avoiding the centre, look up the little streets to the left and catch glimpses of the old town and the blue dome of the small church. Climb out of the valley, through some vineyards, cross over the motorway, and turn right on the N332 to Calpe. As you descend through more vineyards, flat-topped Oltá (Walk 3) and the rugged Bernia Ridge become prominent on the right, and the Penyal d'Ifach (photograph page 19) comes into view ahead. Take the left turn to Calpe Norte (134km ☎), back to the Plaza Central, where the tour began (135km).

4 SOUTHERN VALLEYS AND WESTERN HIGHLANDS

Benidorm • Sella • Penáguila • Alcoi • Cocentaina • Bocairent • Coves de Canalobre • Benidorm

215km/133mi; 5 hours' driving; exit A from Benidorm (plan page 8)

On route: ⊞ at Penáguila, Font Roja, Cocentaina; Picnics (see **P** symbol and pages 10-15): 18a-c, 19-22, 23a, 23b; Walks 4, 14, 17-23

From fertile valleys and heavily-wooded hillsides to desert wastes and stark peaks — this tour takes you through all manner of landscapes. Castles, caves and prehistoric paintings are just some of the features en route, and there are frequent opportunities to leave your car. Apart from exploring the interesting settlements it takes you through, we suggest several short strolls to the features of interest. To do and see everything would be too much for one day, so consider taking two days for this tour.

Take exit A from Benidorm, signposted to Alicante, and follow the signs to the Carrefour supermarket, where the tour starts. From the supermarket continue on the CV767, making straight for the hills — the Cortina Ridge, with the notch of Campana standing out prominently behind it. Pass **Finestrat** (5km ✕), its houses perched precariously on a hillside, and circle clockwise to a minor crossroads, then turn left towards Sella on the CV758. (A right turn would take you to the parking for Walk 4.) This road climbs below Campana, affording good views of the 'shark's teeth' of El Realet. Benidorm is soon forgotten, as high-rise blocks and fancy villas give way to spectacular mountain peaks and grand old *fincas*.

At the T-junction (13km) turn right and head towards Penya Sella — a long flat ridge ending with three peaks on the right. Climb steeply above a *barranco* and terracing and go through **Sella** (17km ✕), noticing the contrast in vegetation on the slopes on either side of you — barren old almond terraces on the right-hand (sunny) side and dense woods on the left. Just as the road sweeps left (23km), a road with PR waymarking rises to the right. Walk 14 which traverses the Penya Sella Ridge starts 5km up this road. Continuing on the CV770 as it climbs steeply, ignore a left turn to Relleu. The antennas up on the right signal Aitana — Alicante's highest mountain. At a fork (27km) go left for 'Safari Aitana', 'Seguro', 'Penáguila' (CV785). The road climbs high above the valleys, an eye-catching panorama spread before you, and then levels out before passing the Safari Park★ entrance (33km).

Now gradually descending the far side of the hill, you pass through heavily wooded terrain, which continues until the next valley opens out. On the far side of the rocky crag ahead are the remains of Penáguila Castle (Walk 22). Pass the gates of El Coyao on the left (37km **P**22; Short walk 22). From this point the road winds down into **Penáguila** (41km ⬙✝✕⌂) and then bears left towards Benifallím. On the next sharp right-hand bend, it is worth stopping to look behind you, where the the view of the castle and a natural rock arch (the Arco de Santa Llúcia) will long remain in your memory.

Further along you pass the Mas de Pau *hostal* and adjacent *ermita* on the right (43km ▲✝). As you round another bend, Benifallím comes spectacularly into view, its castle on the left. Go past the village (45km) and follow the road towards Alcoi. It undulates through pleasant scenery to a T-junction at a bridge (52km ✕), where you turn right on the N340 (✕). In the background, the Barranc del Sinc slices through the rocky cliff face.

At traffic lights on the outskirts of **Alcoi**★ (55km ✝▲▲ ✕⌂⊕M⌨), you can take an optional detour (signposted slip road on the right; 18km return) to the Santuario de la Font Roja★ (✝✕⌂△**P**21). This natural park, high in the mountains, is the setting for Walk 21 and well worth a visit. The main tour goes straight on at the lights, following the one-way system and signs to Valencia on the N340, winding all the way through Alcoi. This fascinating town, below the sheer cliffs of the Barranc del Sinc, has two centres, connected by huge bridges. You will surely want to delve into its history and explore its older quarters. Eventually you find yourself on the tree-lined Avinguda l'Alameda, where you will cross a bridge over the Barranc del Sinc (58km). Just *before* the bridge, the supermarket Mercadona on the right is the starting point for Walk 18. But motorists can drive much closer to the fabulous setting shown on page 103 (**P**18a) by following the *walking notes* on page 101.

Continue over the bridge and, on leaving Alcoi, you will see Cocentaina Castle prominent ahead on its rocky pinnacle; Montcabrer (Walk 18), the main peak of the Serra de Mariola rises majestically on the left. Drive through **Cocentaina** (63km ✝▲▲✕⌂⊕⌂) and, at the roundabout just before leaving the town, notice a road going left to the castle (⬙) and the Sant Cristófol *zona recreativa* (✕⌂**P**18b-c).

Some 6km from Cocentaina take the slip road signposted to Muro and Agres (CV700). Turn left towards Agres and cross the pine-clad slopes of the Agres Valley. After going under the railway (75km), climb gradually until Agres comes into view on the left. Above the village, clinging to the hillside, is the Ermita de la Mare de Deu (**P**19) which Walk 19 passes on its way to the refuge and the *cavas* (snow wells). Just after the 8km road marker, at a signposted crossroads, turn sharp left (76km) and drive up to **Agres** (77km ✝▲▲✕). Turn left at the fork and wind up through the narrow streets of this interesting village. Continuing straight on at the crossroads (78km) would take you up Carrer Major to the church where Walk 19 starts, but the tour turns *right* into Carrer San Antonio. Pass Pensión Mariola and, at the end of the street (at the railings) turn sharp right and head back down to the main road. Turn left and continue west. As the road descends gently, look up to the left and see if you can spot Cava Gran, a circular stone building on top of the ridge; it is visited on Walk 19.

Drive through **Alfafara** (82km) passing two old *fincas* on the right, their terraced fields still well cultivated. Turn left at the T-junction (86km) signposted to Villena (CV81), and soon have magnificent views of the old town of **Bocairent★** (✝▲▲✕🅿⊕M🎦), with its *ermita* high on a hill to the right. The town, shown opposite, is worth exploring: turn right (88km) at a roundabout, following 'Bocairent', and go over a bridge. Follow the one-way system and signs to museums and the tourist office. You climb high into the village, to the large oval Plaza de la Ajuntament (89km). This houses the tourist office and museum. From here you can walk along a lane to the Covetes de los Moros★, described and illustrated on page 98. Short walk 17 will take you there, while the main walk (illustrated on page 96) goes along an old mule trail to Ontinyent. Both walks begin at the tourist office.

From the square, follow the signs directing you back to the CV81 and, after crossing the bridge, turn right towards the petrol station (🅿). Go straight on at a round-about and loop right for the left turn on the CV794, with a campsite sign. Not far along the road (91km) turn left towards the signposted campsite. The road (CV794) winds high above the Agres Valley on to a wooded plateau. Across the plateau the land opens out and several small farmhouses lie amongst the cultivated fields. After entering the woods once more, Mariola Castle appears ahead on a rocky peak. Just past the 9km road marker (100km Δ) you pass on the left the entrance to the commercial campsite previously signposted. Beyond a small bridge, an unsurfaced road up to the left is signposted 'Font de Mariola — Area Recreativa'. If you would like a break, turn up here and park near the building which serves as a shelter for campers and picnickers. This is Font Mariola's free camping area, with picnic benches and a *font* (△⛺*P*20). Walk 20, to Alt de la Cova, begins here and, just past the benches, Short walk 20-2 leads up a track through pines to Mariola Castle. Returning to the road, turn left and after a few kilometres wind down across a narrow bridge. On reaching a crest, look ahead to the thickly-wooded slopes: you can see the Font Roja sanctuary. To the left and slightly lower down is Barxell Castle.

Wind down into **El Barxell** (109km) and, at the junction, cross the bridge and turn right towards Banyeres (CV795). Within 300m pass a dirt road off to the left which leads to Barxell Castle, a five minute walk away. The road continues across the plain, through well-cultivated farmlands and past El Altet, another old *finca* on the right. Turn left towards Ibi on the CV801 (116km) and climb through fertile terraces, ignoring a right turn to Onil. This Castalla/Onil/Ibi area produces almost all the toys and dolls for the whole of Spain. From a crest, Ibi can be seen sprawled out in

Bocairent rises above its medieval bridge.

the valley below. The two hills north of the town used to bear castles, but now there are two *ermitas*, one dedicated to Santa Lucia, the other to San Miguel.

Winding downhill you have a good view of the pointed peak of Maigmó ahead. As you approach the factory at the entrance to **Ibi** (125km 🛉✕🏪), notice the two brick gate-posts on the left and a PR signpost. Walk 21 to Font Roja passes through here. Continue into town and, just before reaching the *ajuntament* (town hall, where Walk 21 begins), notice a street to the right: Calle Vicente Pascual. A little way along the street there is an interesting modern fountain — worth a quick visit. Set into its walls are ceramic tiles each bearing a picture — a shield or crest, a castle or *ermita*, all with some connection with Ibi.

Continue by turning left at the *ajuntament* and go straight on at the petrol station (🏪) junction on the CV806 for Alcoi. After passing large expanses of cultivated fields, reach a roundabout. Follow the signs for the A7 to Alcoi and do the same at a second roundabout. You are now on the A7 *autovía*. Take the first exit to Xixona (135km) and join the N340 south. This road crosses a high pass, and signs will tell you if it is open. But first, just after turning right, take a little road to the left signposted to **La Sarga**. Drive about 0.5km through apple orchards to this small collection of houses, then leave them on the right: take the *camino rural* (136km), which soon sweeps to the left over the *barranco* and winds up to Mas de la Cova (**P**23b). Ahead in the rock face, just a short walk away, are caves with prehistoric paintings.

Return to the main road, turn left, and wind up to the **Port de la Carrasqueta**, a pass at 1020m/3350ft. Park at the *mirador* (144km 📷) and take in the surrounding views. Walk 23 to Pou del Surdo (**P**23a; photograph page 119) and the Carrasqueta Ridge starts here. Over the pass the road winds down through steep hairpins, with ample places to pull over and take in yet more stunning views (📷). On the downhill stretch (🏪 at 150 km and several ✕), you pass an *ermita* (155km) and soon see the distinctive split peak of Penya Roja which towers over Xixona.

A bypass avoids the town, but drive into **Xixona** (157km 🛉🔺✕🏪⊕M), the confectionery capital of Spain. Its situation in the centre of the almond-growing region determines its importance in the *turrón* (nougat) industry — it even has a museum of *turrón!* Unless you wish to explore the town, turn left (signposted to Alicante) and

continue through the barren waste that the lan
around Xixona has become after years of drought. C
sional sproutings of vegetation in the dry river beds
evidence of some underground water — oases in wha
otherwise essentially desert. About 3km south of Xixona
at the 764km marker (161km), turn left on the CV774,
signposted to Busot. This fairly rough, narrow road snakes
downhill, crosses a bridge over a dry river bed and later,
near the 3km marker, winds up to Toll del Carmello —
where a pair of reservoirs comes as a surprise (169km).

Shortly after this, turn left uphill (170km) towards the
Serra del Cabeço d'Or. Situated at over 700m/2300ft, the
Coves de Canalobre★ (175km **M**), with magnificent
stalactites and stalagmites, are considered the most important in the Valencian region. They were used originally for cold storage, but in the Spanish Civil War they
served as an arms depot. Rather incongruously, there is
also an American Indian Museum alongside the caves.
Even if you do not visit the caves, take a few minutes to
admire the spectacular view (⌑) over the valley.

From the caves return to the road, turn left (180km)
and drive through **Busot** (182km). The notice 'Comparsa
Els Contrabandistes' ('Smugglers' Group') above the door
of a little house just before the post office has us
wondering if this might have been an old smuggling town.
At the main junction in the village, turn left for Aigües de
Busot (CV773; not signposted until *after* you turn off) and
climb through yet more hairpins round the rocky
mountainside, before descending to the next junction
(188km). Turn left on the CV775 to **Aigües de Busot**
(191km **▲▲✕M**). This is a spa town, busy at weekends.
Follow the signs to Relleu, but after 2km turn right
(193km) for La Vila Joiosa.

This delightful narrow road undulates straight towards
Campana, with the antennas of Aitana high on the left. At
every turn and crest new beauties of nature come into
focus; then the man-made Presa de Amadorio appears on
the left (202km). Go through a tunnel, cross the wall of
this huge reservoir and almost immediately overlook La
Vila Joiosa. Pass its sports centre on the left (205km) and,
50m further on, turn right at the T-junction. This road
takes you through orange groves and into **La Vila Joiosa**
(**╆▲▲✕☗⊕△**). While still short of the centre, turn left
(207km), following signposting for Benidorm. Skirt round
the edge of the town, to a major junction (209km). Turn
(N332) and drive back into Benidorm (215km).

n/86mi; 3 hours' driving. Exit A from Alicante (plan page 9). From
where, join the tour at the A7 junction, just east of the A31.
proaching Elda, use the large-scale map on the reverse of the touring
ap for help with navigation if you are going to one of the walks.
On route: 🛱 at Novelda; Picnics (see **P** symbol and pages 10-15): 24,
25a, 25b; Walks: 24, 25, 26

*The province of Alicante played an important role in the history of the
region during the seven or eight centuries of the Reconquest from the
Moors. This role can be appreciated as you consider the vast number
of castles which remain today, some in ruins, others well preserved or
restored. One of the best known figures associated with the period must
be El Cid, the legendary 11th-century mercenary considered at the time
to be a national patriot. The town and the mountain named after him
feature prominently on this tour.*

From the roundabout at the RENFE railway station, head
for the A31 to Madrid, driving towards the stark
mounds of the Serra de Fontcalent. Continue past the A7
junction (4km 🚗) and after 1km join the A31 (🚗 16km).
Beyond the Portitxol Pass (🚗 20km) and shortly after
another petrol station, take the slip road to **Monforte del
Cid** (22km ⬜🕆🚗). This town, said to be one of the two
oldest settlements in the province, merits a visit. A church
with a striking blue ceramic dome now stands on the old
fortifications, its bell tower fashioned from one of the
ancient defensive towers.

Follow signs for Madrid and Albacete to return to the
A31, then turn off to **Novelda** (27km ⬜🕆M). Its main
products are table grapes and saffron, but its main attrac-
tion is its castle. After crossing the river turn off right
(signed to Murcia), then right again (signed to the Castell
de la Mola). This road leads to the castle in about 1km.
There is ample parking space (34km). As you approached
it was probably not the castle, but the impressive Santuario de la Magdalena which caught your eye. It is ornately
arabesque and dates from 1912. The castle itself has been
declared a national monument and is in the process of
being restored. You will have noticed picnic benches (🛱)
below the car park, but a better place to relax is at the top
of the hill behind the sanctuary, where more benches
afford a magnificent view over Aspe and Novelda.

Drive back into Novelda, turn left at the gardens, and
then follow signs to Elda, to get back on the A31. Behind
the pointed hill on your right, you have your first view of
the impressive El Cid, its twin peaks joined by a lor
shallow plateau. This view improves as you drive throu
the still-barren terrain and take the exit for **Elda** (4

☐✝⛰✕🚻⊕M). This large town has a chequered past 1304 it passed from the kingdom of Castilla to that Valencia and, after the expulsion of the Muslims in 1609, it was left deserted. Castellanos eventually repopulated the area, imposing their language (Spanish as we know it), despite the fact that all around, even one street away in Petrer, the people spoke Valenciano. As you drive through, follow signs for Sax on the CV833.

Elda railway station is the starting point for Walk 24 which leads to the huge sand dune shown on page 123 and down a fascinating old trail along a watercourse. Continue on the west side of the Viñalopó River (CV833) to **Sax** (59km 🚉). Its name derives from the Latin *saxum*, meaning large boulder. Turn right at the first roundabout, go straight on at the second roundabout and drive through the town, round the right-hand side of the castle which sits on this 500m/1650ft-high boulder. It was built first by the Romans; reconstructed by the Arabs in the eighth century, it has one Roman and one Arabic tower. As you drive round the back, past the wooded slopes, you can park beside a gate and enter the grounds on foot. A short walk round the castle offers a good view of the surrounding countryside, cultivated with almonds and olives.

Leaving the castle behind, continue uphill and across a bridge. At the roundabout (where you cross the railway and then the *autovía*), go straight on for Castalla, joining the CV80 *autovía*. On the left you will see the antennas on top of Penya Rossa and the flat-topped ridge of the Serra del Frare (Walk 26); to the right is the Serra de l'Arguenya. Continue to the exit for Castalla and Biar (70km). At the top of the slip road, go straight on at the roundabout for Castalla. (Walk 26 starts 8km up the road to the left here, in Biar.) The first town you see to the left is Onil, but then Castalla Castle appears on the right, the view becoming ever more magnificent as you draw nearer. Drive round its base to **Castalla** (76km ☐✝✕🚻). The town's name derives from the Latin *castra alta* or high castle, for obvious reasons. It has not been completely restored, but is worth a visit. The town also has a baroque church dating from 1613, an *ermita* and an 18th-century convent. Go straight ahead at the traffic lights, passing the church on your right. As you leave town notice bar-'iscotheque Triangulo set off the road on the left then 'n right into Calle Manuel de Falla. Turn right at the T-'ction, first left (Dr Fleming) then left again into enida de Petrer (CV817), heading towards the crags of espeñador.

Go left at a fork, following a 'Xorret de Catí' sign (a hotel; 78km); 300m to the *right* at this fork is the starting point for Walk 25 (***P***25a), a long, varied hike which takes in the summit of Despeñador. Keeping left, drive through extensive almond and olive groves towards the hills, then wind up steeply through pines until you are directly under Despeñador. The road takes you round to the left and up to a crest. The twin peaks of El Cid stand out ahead as you descend into the valley, where Xorret de Catí is visible below. Be careful here — you may encounter walkers on the road. At a junction (86km) follow the sign to Petrer and Elda. Pass the **Catí** hotel tennis courts and stop at the front entrance. You can avail yourself of the hotel facilities (✕▲) or stretch your legs. Alternative walk 25-3 starts here, and walkers' signpost PR-V29 points the way to the Ermita de Catí (***P***25b).

Continue from the hotel entrance, turn left past the car park, and go straight on at a 'Stop' sign. You soon descend steeply into a dip where the Pantanet Gorge is off to the right (Walk 25). Continue up out of the dip for a view of the gorge. Pass Casa Pantanet and, at a junction (91km), turn right. (A left turn would take you to the foot of El Cid.) Continue the descent and, after a little more than 1km, look for a drystone wall on the left. This surrounds an old two-tier *era* (threshing floor), with its cylindrical millstone still in place. Shortly after this (93km) you see the beginnings of La Rambla dels Molins on the left, the watercourse on the route of Walks 24 and 25. Follow this past Restaurante Molino la Roja (✕ start of Short walk 24-1, ***P***24), then drive high above the *rambla,* taking in its spectacular rock formations.

As you round a bend, Petrer Castle comes into sight. The tiny Carrer de las Casitas ('Street of the Little Houses') leading up to this Arabic castle is picturesque, and the castle itself is almost fully restored. Stop at the *mirador* (97km 📷) for a longer look; notice, too, the twin towns of Elda and Petrer and more views of El Cid. Wind downhill and, if you want to explore another town, turn right into **Petrer** (♜✝▲✕⛽⊕). Otherwise, go under the *autovía,* past Carrefour hypermarket, do a U-turn at the roundabout and go on to the A31 signposted to Alicante/ Alacant. Pass the A7 junction (132km) and follow sig to the centre of Alicante. These will lead you back to station roundabout (138km).

✿Walking

While the car tours take you through spectacular country-side, it is really only when walking that you can fully appreciate the beauty of this landscape. From a car you would not notice the fish swimming contentedly in the clear and sparkling water of a mountain stream, the clump of orchids at the side of a path, the relentless call of the corn bunting or the sweet smell of rosemary. We hope that what you do see on your car tours will entice you to walk. *There are walks here for everyone to enjoy.*

As you will notice from any high vantage point, the mountains in the Costa Blanca region are criss-crossed by a myriad of tracks and paths. Some of these, used for centuries by farmers and shepherds, connect remote settlements and villages and provide access to *fincas, fonts* and fields. Others are more recent, sometimes the result of quarrying and forestry activities. The replace-ment of donkey and mule by tractor and trailer has resulted in many paths being widened into tracks and, in some cases, surfaced roads. Our walks follow footpaths wherever possible, but often tracks are unavoidable. However, these tracks are so little used that they should not spoil your enjoyment of the walks.

The area is well walked, and there are some classic routes, parts of which we have included. But we have, for example, rejected or adapted those which involve nothing more than a sheer slog to the summit of a mountain and back down again. In an attempt to tailor our walks specifically for users of *Landscapes* books, and taking into account the region's limited public transport service, we have tried to provide circular, rather than out-and-back walks. In order to make this possible we some-times include short stretches on asphalt roads. But these are always quiet country roads, generally free of traffic.

If you are walking on a Sunday or a *fiesta,* choose as remote a location as you can find. That is the day when Spaniards pack up their cars and head for the wide open spaces — to hunt, to gather wild mushrooms, to collect water from mountain *fonts,* to picnic or simply to enjoy a drive. Roads will be busy, and picnic sites with benches and car access could well be chock-a-block.

Unless you are doing one of the walks close to the

39

tourist beat, the accepted greeting for other walkers or for farmers is the Valenciano *Bon día*, rather than the Spanish *Buenos días*. It will always elicit a hearty response.

It is important that all walkers read and *heed* the country code on page 11.

G rading and timing

When **grading** each walk, we have tried to describe the effort required, the state of the paths, and the ease of navigation. You need not be an expert or even a habitual walker to tackle most of our walks, but a reasonable level of fitness and stamina, as well as some mountain 'sense', is assumed. *Be sure to read through the whole description of a walk before setting out,* so that you know *exactly* what to expect and what to take with you. **If the main walk looks too strenuous for you**, see if there are any short or alternative versions which are less demanding. You need look no further than the picnic suggestions on pages 10-15 to find a wide selection of **very easy walks.**

Despite being in our fifties, *we tend to walk faster than most,* except perhaps on tricky descents. Please compare your pace with ours on one or two short walks, *before* setting out on a long hike. You may have to adjust our timings to suit your own pace — remember this when planning bus or train connections. We give **frequent time checks**. They are *not* meant to be followed minute-by-minute throughout the walk, but to indicate the easily-monitored **time difference** between various points. Check our notes frequently, to avoid missing turn-offs or landmarks. Our **overall timings *do not include any stops.*** Allow time for lunch, photography, bird-watching and botanising. Take account of the weather, too. Hot sun, driving rain and strong winds can affect your rate of progress.

W aymarking and maps

Some of the tourist offices will, if pressed, provide a pamphlet (normally in Spanish) about walks in their area. *But beware!* These are pictorial and very pretty, but usually devoid of description and detail. At best you will find them almost impossible to follow; at worst they could get you completely lost and into some dangerous terrain.

We are confident that you will find the instructions for walks in this book both clear and comprehensive. Some of the paths are not **waymarked** at all. Others have been marked by local walking groups. You will see the red and white striped waymarks of the GR7 ('Gran Recorrid long-distance footpath and, increasingly, the yellow and white stripes and signposts for PR ('Pequeño Recorrido') short-distance walks. Elsewhere there may be coloured dots, arrows or cairns — or a combination of all of these. Our walks often coincide with waymarked routes but seldom follow them all the way — *so don't get carried away by the markings; read our instructions.*

Our **maps**, based on Spanish military surveys (1970s-80s), have been thoroughly updated for this book. They were correct at press date but, as more of the countryside is exploited, new tracks or roads are likely to appear. All our suggested routes are highlighted in green (or mauve for alternatives), and *we would advise you to stick to these.* You can buy 1:50,000 or 1:25,000 maps of the area from your usual stockist, but beware: they *do* contain errors and are rarely up to date.

W here to stay

If you take a package holiday you will undoubtedly find yourself in one of the **coastal towns**. If travelling independently and keen to walk, you might prefer to stay **in the mountains**, where there are a few *pensiones* and *hostales* (some English-run). Even in the smallest villages there may be someone willing to offer you basic hospitality. Tourist offices provide a list of accommodation, but it is by no means complete — village bars are a better source of advice. There are **campsites** in Vall d'Alcalá (good facilities, uninspiring site), Vall d'Ebo (basic but grassy, with plenty of trees), Font Mariola (both a huge commercial site, with all facilities, and, less than 1km away, a much more attractive, free municipal site, with a *font*), and Font Roja (reasonable facilities and no charge). On the coast, a site we have *not* visited is near Campello harbour (www.campingcostablanca.com).

W eather

With care, you can walk comfortably in this region all year round — as long as you **heed the weather signs and carry appropriate equipment**. The best time to walk is undoubtedly spring, when the hillsides are carpeted with a huge variety of colourful and delicate flowers and herbs — providing a feast for butterflies and birds and a great spectacle for walkers. But the limestone rock and the nature of the climate ensures that you will find some flowers in bloom in the mountains at any time of year.

There can be **frost** in the mountains in winter with **snow** on the highest peaks and **strong winds** in exposed areas may make it feel very cold sometimes. February and November can be quite wet; **heavy storms**, which cause damage to tracks and paths, often occur in September and early October. Such storms, though not usually very long-lasting, can be quite unexpected and frighteningly fierce, so make sure you are prepared. The strength of the **sun** should not be ignored at any time of the year, and it can be blisteringly hot from May to October.

What to take

The mountains of the Costa Blanca are unlikely to present the sort of extreme weather conditions that might be encountered at home but, nevertheless, you should equip yourself for all eventualities. The sun can be strong at any time of the year, so **suncream, sunhat and long-sleeved shirt** should always be taken with you on walks. According to the season and prevailing weather conditions, you must judge what **extra items of clothing** you might need. Storms *can* occur in summer, and even on a bright sunny day it can be very chilly at high altitude — so take **warm and waterproof clothing** on mountain walks. The whole area tends to be very rocky underfoot and **stout, thick-soled shoes, preferably with ankle support, are a must for all but one or two of the walks.** Unless you are walking in extremely bad weather you should not require heavy boots, but for comfort we certainly recommend lightweight hiking boots or shoes. Paths and tracks can be very muddy for a day or so after

Walk 1: On the descent from Montgó, we meet some walkers climbing to the summit. Xábia lies below. Most of the paths on this walk are rocky and, while wide enough to be comfortable, they demand care.

heavy rain, with the clay-like soil clinging to your boots. The other essential is **water**. Bottled water is widely available. There are *fonts* on a few of the walks but in summer months you are quite likely to find they are dry. For all longer walks you should take a **picnic lunch**.

For each walk, we specify any additional items you will require. We have sometimes included **compass** directions as extra confirmation of the route to take. Although all the walks can be followed without a compass it would be foolish to tackle any of the high mountain ones without one, since mist or cloud can soon obliterate landmarks and lead to disorientation.

For **emergencies** it is always wise to carry a **first-aid kit,** some high energy food, extra water, a couple of large black plastic bags, whistle, compass, torch and some warm clothing.

N uisances
Dogs might be encountered as you pass close to farms, but they are usually chained up or fenced in and when they're loose they seldom present a threat. However, the sudden noise of their barking as they sense an alien presence can give you a fright and if they do bound out of a gateway straight towards you, you should slow down but continue on your way without showing panic or aggression. If dogs worry you, invest in a 'Dog Dazer', an ultrasonic dog deterrent. Contact Sunflower Books, who sell them (www.sunflowerbooks.co.uk).

It is unlikely that you will have a problem with either **snakes** or **scorpions**, but you should be aware of the possibility — greater if you are just a couple of walkers proceeding quietly. In warm weather we see snakes quite regularly, usually slithering out of our way at the side of a path, disturbed by our approach. The only poisonous snake is a viper with a triangular yellowish head and a zigzag line down its spine. A bite from one of these needs urgent medical attention. Scorpion stings should also be treated quickly. But you will avoid problems if you are careful: keep to the path, do not disturb rocks or stones, and think twice before sitting on a drystone wall.

O rganisation of the walks
The area covered by this guide is bounded by the coast in the east, the Serra de Benicadell in the north, the serras of Mariola and Maigmó in the west, and the city of Alicante in the south. This inverted triangle includes a

very complex topography, with over 35 named serras, both rugged and gentle, interspersed by a large number of picturesque valleys. This complexity makes for fascinating and varied walking, but makes it difficult to group the walks in a simple way.

We have chosen to split the walks into six groups, categorised by the coastal strip in the east, the serras forming the western border of the area, and those based around groups of valleys going roughly west to east:

Walks 1-5: coastal strip from Dénia to Benidorm
Walks 6-9: Serpis and Gallinera valleys
Walks 10-12: Laguar and Jalón valleys
Walks 13-16: Guadalest, Algar and Sella valleys
Walks 17-22: Alcoi area
Walks 23-26: serras of Carrasqueta and Maigmó

You will probably start with walks closest to where you are based, but all are quite accessible from any of the coastal resorts. You'll find an overview of the walk areas on the fold-out touring map, and a quick flip through the book will reveal at least one photograph for each walk.

Finally, we would like to **highlight five walks** which will give you a good cross-section of the terrain and landscape. **Walk 1** takes you to a mountain summit; **Walk 6** leads along a beautiful river valley and up to a castle; **Walk 10** traverses amazing Mozarabic trails from the Middle Ages; **Walk 13** follows some gentle mountain valleys under the highest mountain in Alicante province; and **Walk 19** visits 17th-century 'snow wells' (*cavas*) on a high mountain ridge.

Each description begins with planning information: times and distances, grade, equipment and how to get there. For some of the main walks we suggest possible alternatives and give a short version wherever feasible. Before the detailed description of the route there is a general introduction to give you a 'feel' for the landscape.

Below is a key to the **symbols** on the walking maps:

▬▬▬	motorway	●→	spring *(font)*, well, etc	☗†	church, chapel.shrine
▬▬▬	dual carriageway	**P**	picnic suggestion (see pages 10-15)	○	charcoal burners' terrace, limekiln
▬▬▬	main road	🖘	best views	▣	watchtower
────	secondary road	🚌	bus stop	⊡	cemetery
────	narrow road	🚃	railway station	⊼	picnic tables
▦▦▦	unmade road, street	�"	car parking	⋏	transmitter.pylon
────	jeep track, etc	■□	building.enclosure	△	rock formation
-------	path, steps	■▯	castle or fort.ruined	☼	mill
₂→	main walk	⚒	quarry, mine	≶	electricity sub-station
₂→	alternative walk	∩	cave	●	snow well

1 MONTGO

See also Dénia plan on page 9 and photographs on pages 11 and 42

Distance: 13km/8mi; 5h48min

Grade: quite strenuous, with a climb and descent of 640m/2100ft on good, but rocky paths. You must be surefooted and have a head for heights. Navigation is straightforward throughout. Avoid windy days.

Equipment: see page 42; also walking boots with ankle support, compass, extra water in summer

How to get there and return: 🚗 to/from Montgó Natural Park (see Car tour 1 at the 93km-point). Or on foot from the Alqueries railway station: walk up Camí del Pou de la Montanya, just next to the station; it's signposted to the park and the Ermita Pare Pere (add about 20min walk each way; see plan on page 9).

Short walk: Cova de l'Aigua. 3.5km/2.2mi; 1h. Easy. Equipment as page 42. Access/return as main walk. Follow the main walk to the 19min-point and turn left. A few minutes later take the marked path on the right to the Cova de l'Aigua. Return the same way.

Alternative walk: Cova de l'Aigua and Cova del Camell. 11km/6.8mi; 3h30min. Easy. Equipment as page 42. Access/return as main walk. Follow the short walk to the Cova de l'Aigua, but turn right when you come back down to the Camí de la Colonia (43min). Continue as far as the Cova del Camell (1h55min) and return the same way.

The Parque Natural del Montgó takes its name from the forbidding-looking mountain shown on page 11, which forms the backdrop to the resorts of Dénia and Xábia. This walk ascends its northeast face, descends south towards Xábia, then skirts the foot of the mountain on an old trail.

Start out at the ENTRANCE to the **Parque Natural**: take the track behind the chain barrier. It zigzags up the lower slopes to the old trail, the **Camí de la Colonia** (19min), which contours round the foot of Montgó. Turn right (you will return from the left, and *the Short and Alternative walks turn left now*). The humidity on this face of the mountain encourages the growth of lush ferns, but has not prevented fires. When the trail peters out (31min), turn sharp left on a path which begins to climb quite steeply as it approaches a sheer cliff. A short level stretch under the cliff offers a brief respite (56min), just before you meet another narrow path coming up from the Cova de l'Aigua.

Fork right here (1h03min) and head uphill again on a steep, rocky path lined with wild flowers, keeping a careful watch for the YELLOW/WHITE WAYMARKS. Just before a crest (1h28min), a path comes in from the right, by a cairn. This is one of the other routes up the mountain, via the Penya del Aguila, and if you are very lucky you may see the eagles (*águilas*) after which the Penya is named.

From the crest head left on an obvious path lined with lavender and rosemary. Eventually (2h05min) a clear path marked with stones leads left to a large cross (**Cruz** del Montgó) on a peak, but this is *not* the true summit. Keep straight ahead with the the YELLOW/WHITE WAY-MARKS. Your path, sometimes narrow and exposed, snakes along to a lone pine and a cave, and then up to the TOP OF **Montgó** (753m/2470ft; **2h45min**). Inland the serras unfold layer by layer; along the coast, you can see as far as Gandía to the north and Calpe to the south. On a clear day Ibiza is visible on the eastern horizon.

Looking inland, your descent path lies over to the left, within five metres of the summit, heading a little east of south. Clear RED PAINT MARKS guide you: the first section is a bit of a scramble down the rocky slope. The scramble ends (**3h12min**) and you join the well-built path shown on page 42, which zigzags all the way down the middle slopes. As you get lower, look down and locate your goal: a clear, wide path, originating in a *barranco* and winding round the foot of the mountain to the left.

Just after a short uphill section, Xábia comes into view ahead. Ignore all the steep short-cut paths through the thickening vegetation, so as not to miss the YELLOW WAY-MARKS on the left (**4h**) which indicate your route to Dénia. They lead you over the rocks and along the right bank of a *barranco,* to a path from where the holding wall of the wide path you saw from above is visible. Descend into the *barranco,* passing the **Cova del Camell** (**4h13min**).

Cross the *barranco* and climb to the path above, the **Camí de la Colonia**. Flat and beautifully constructed, it provides ever-changing views over the coast. After passing an old KILN and a CISTERN, you will meet another, dauntingly steep, route up to the summit. Beyond two more CISTERNS and a RUINED HOUSE, you pass the steep signposted PATH UP TO THE COVA DE L'AIGUA (**5h25min**), an impressive natural cavity with a permanent spring, which in the past provided much of Dénia's water. (Allow an extra 20min return for this detour.) Continue on the *camí* to the junction with your outward track (**5h30min**). Turn right downhill, back to the PARK ENTRANCE (**5h48min**).

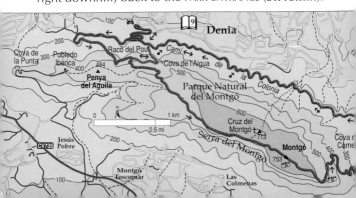

2 SHORT WALKS AROUND XÁBIA AND CALPE

Equipment for all walks: see page 42; also swimming gear for Walks 2c-d. Trainers should suffice as footwear.

Distance, grade, access: see individual walks.

a   Cap de Sant Antoni. 4km/2.5mi; 1h34min. Easy. By 🚌 or on foot to the port at the northern end of Xábia. See text below.

b   Los Molinos. 5km/3mi; 1h23min (with detour 7km/4.3mi; 2h19min). The main walk is an easy stroll; the optional detour is very steep and strenuous and requires great care. 🚌 to the *zona recreativa* on the Cap de Sant Antoni road (see Car tour 1 from about 76km). Ample parking and 🍴, water taps; pleasantly set amidst pines. See text page 48.

c   Cap Prim. 2km/1.2mi; 35min. Easy. 🚌 to the Creu del Portitxol, a stone cross on the CV742 (the 55km-point on Car tour 1). Pick up text on page 49. **See photograph page 11.**

d   Calpe cliffs and *calas*. 6km/3.8mi; 1h48min. Easy. 🚐 bus or 🚌 car to the 30km point of Car tour 1, or walk to Cala Calalga at the eastern end of Calpe's promenade, just beyond the Hotel Esmeralda.

These four short walks provide a good cross-section of coastal scenery in this delightful area. The secluded coves, rugged headlands and old windmills capture the beauty of the landscape around Xábia and Calpe.

Start Walk a at the PORT in **Xábia**: follow the coast road past the RED CROSS BUILDING. Just beyond the CLUB NAUTICO, when the road ends (**6min**), go up some concrete steps to the left. These give way to a narrow rocky PATH, MARKED IN RED, which snakes up the hillside. At a fork, go left, along the left-hand side of a *barranco*. Cross this stream bed (**19min**) and turn right along its far bank, heading east towards Cap de Sant Antoni. Here you lose the waymarking. At **25min** ignore a path downhill to the right and continue gently climbing. In spring the scent of rosemary and pine mingle tantalisingly, and in autumn the slopes are clad with heather. The clear path contours round the slopes, circles the head of another *barranco* (**34min**) and eventually forks (**46min**). The right fork goes to the lighthouse on the headland at Cap de Sant Antoni. Take the left fork, which leads you up to a CAR PARK and *mirador* with a water tap on the main Cap de Sant Antoni road (**49min**). From here you have a fantastic view down to Xábia. Cap de Sant Antoni is 200m away to the right. To the left, eight minutes' walk away, is a *zona recreativa* where you could link up with the start of Walk 2b. Otherwise, retrace your steps back to the PORT (**1h34min**).

Start Walk b at the *zona recreativa* on the CAP DE SANT ANTONI ROAD: take the wide chained-off gravel track which heads off to the left just before the benches. Follow it until, at **20min**, you reach a T-junction with an old

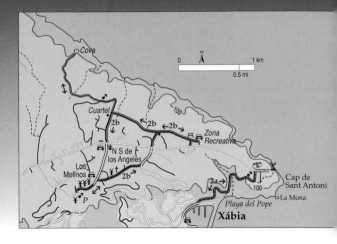

abandoned *cuartel* (military barracks) just off to the left.
Turn left*, pass the *cuartel* and some villas, and reach the
main Cap de Sant Antoni road (**25min**). Cross the road
and walk up CAMI DEL MONASTIR, which follows the
boundary walls of an imposing *santuario*. This narrow
cypress-lined road is asphalted at first but soon becomes
unsurfaced. As it sweeps left (you will return this way
later) go straight ahead (**31min**) and you will see the FIRST
WINDMILL *(molino)* at the top of the crest just in front.

More mills are lined up along the crest, all but one —
twelve in all. First visit the mills to the right. Take the path
going up to the first mill and continue along past the
others, some of which are now privately owned and
which you skirt round on a path on the Xábia side of the
cliff. A narrow asphalt road (**41min**) takes you the
remaining few metres to the path up to the last three in
this line of mills (**46min**), from where the views are
spectacular (**P**2b; photograph page 50). The mills were
positioned to catch the best of the winds, vital for the
grinding of the grain grown long ago on the terraces. It is
over a hundred years since they were last in use, but only
one of them is a complete ruin. The towers of the rest
remain solid although they have all lost their cones and
sails.

Retrace your steps to the point where you reached the
crest (**55min**). The path which runs downward below the

*If you are surefooted and agile, you can take a 1h detour: turn *right*
here. After five minutes, on a left-hand bend (just after a wall), take a
path off to the right, past a *font* and a little water tank. After crossing an
open area it descends very steeply down rocky slopes to a spectacular
cave, almost at sea level. Retrace your steps to the junction.

mills winds its way into Xábia, but you turn left, back towards the *santuario*. After about 100m/yds turn right on the unsurfaced road. This leads past a STONE CROSS and the TWELFTH MILL. Notice the game bird breeding aviary nearby on the left — sadly now out of use — and turn left on the asphalted CALLE CUESTA DE SAN ANTONIO (a right turn here leads down into Xábia port). Cross the main Cap de Sant Antoni road (**1h08min**), go straight ahead and, after 100m/ yds, turn right on a narrow track. This joins your outward track (**1h11min**). Turn right, back to the *zona recreativa* (**1h23min**).

   Start Walk c at the **Creu del Portitxol**: looking out from the cross, you will see the island of Portitxol to the right and the rocky headland of Cap Prim to the left. Directly below, a path winds downhill and then runs alongside some old grassy terraces, beyond which there are pines (**P**2c). Take the path which leads down from the cross, past an information board, but turn sharp left at a junction after only about 30m/yds. Descend through the wooded terraces, passing occasional green and white waymarks. The path takes you to the edge of the cliff, then bears left along the eastern side of the headland. At **9min** the view of Montgó looming ahead is probably the finest you will ever have of that forbidding mountain (shown on page 11). Ignore a path left to Cala Sardinera. This path is very eroded — *don't* be tempted to make your way down any of the shortcuts. Wait till you reach the concrete steps (**45min**) which will take you safely down to **Cala Sardinera** (**P**2c) and continue to the highest point on **Cap Prim** (**19min**). If it is not windy, and you feel brave, you can go a little further out on the sheer rocky promontory but we suggest you just admire the views, before retracing your steps for about 200m/yds to a junction. Take the right fork along the western side of the promontory, passing above Cala Sardinera. Just after rejoining your outward path, pass the route down to Cala Sardinera again and continue back up to the **Creu del Portitxol** (**35min**).

Walk d is an out and back walk, so go as far as you wish. **Start out** at **Cala Calalga**, at the eastern end of the promenade in **Calpe**. Continue northeast, up the road, and turn right on a PR-signposted path to Puerto/Port Bassetes (**4min**). Now what used to be a rather eroded narrow cliff path, with sheer drops to the sea, has been transformed by the construction of flights of steps (some steep), gravelled paths, paved walkways and log fencing. So the nature of this walk has changed, but it still provides stunning views of the Penyal d'Ifach and Cap de Moraira, as well as opportunities to explore tiny *calas* — coves. You pass **Cala el Mallorqui** (**13min**), followed by an interestingly-painted villa and then reach the marina at **Ses Bassetes** (**23min**). From here you go up the steep hill and follow the path alongside the road as far as the **Mirador ses Bassetes** at the 7km marker (**32min**). From the *mirador* the walkway continues on to **Cala Fustera** (**41min**) and **Cala Pinet**. A little further on there is another delightful cove (**54min**; *P*2d). It's secluded, has flat rocks and rock pools, and is an excellent spot to linger awhile.

Return the same way to **Calpe** (**1h48min**).

Los Molinos at Xábia (Picnic 2b and Walk 2b)

3 VUELTA DE OLTA (OLTA CIRCUIT)

See also photograph page 19   **Distance:** 11km/6.8mi; 3h20min

Grade: moderate, with climbs and corresponding descents of about 360m/1180ft overall. Mostly on easy tracks, but surefootedness is essential on a few short sections. The initial climb to the circuit track is steep. Navigation is straightforward; the circuit track has good yellow/white PR waymarking and signposting.

Equipment: see page 42

How to get there and return: 🚌 or 🚗 to Calpe station. Motorists can reduce walking time by about 15min: From Calpe station follow the signs for Monte Olta, Zona de Acampada (3km), where there is a tiny car park. From the campsite a narrow path leads up to a track. Turn left, then 3min later, turn left again at the circuit track. Follow the main walk from the 2h10min-point to the 2h30min-point, then continue on the circuit track by picking up the main walk at the 33min-point.

Alternative walk: Oltá summits. 5km/3mi; 2h10min (plus time to explore the summit). Moderate, with ascents and corresponding descents of 500m/1650ft. Equipment as page 42 plus walking boots; access as main walk. Follow the main walk past the 33min-point and after the sweeping right-hand bend fork *right*. In ten minutes a PR waymarker signals a scramble up a rocky gully. Follow the clear markers all the way up. The gradient eventually eases (1h 01min) and you reach a cairn on the plateau (1h07min), with a large waymark. Just beyond the cairn, paths go left to the southern summit, straight ahead to the northern summit and right to a garishly-painted rock on the eastern face of Oltá. Each is around a 20min walk away. Explore whichever of these routes appeal to you, then retrace your steps back to the information board and down to Calpe station.

This clockwise walk around the Oltá peaks undulates roughly between the 300m and 400m contours. Each time you emerge from the shade of fragrant pine trees you will have spectacular views over Calpe and the coastline or towards the serrated ridges of surrounding serras.

Start out at **Calpe** STATION: cross the RAILWAY LINES just beyond the station, walk up the road a short distance and take a road left (PR sign to Oltá). After about 50m/yds, fork right, heading towards Oltá. Pass a PHONE BOX on your left, go to the top of the hill, then fork right again. Continue on a chained-off forestry road (**8min**). At **15min** fork right once more and, just after, ignore a track coming in from the right. Ignore another track coming in from the right (**20min**). At a three-way junction, where there are fine views ahead to the Serra de Toix (**24min**), go straight on. Ignore a track to the left (**31min**) and reach the CIRCUIT TRACK (**33min**); directly in front of it is a (perhaps empty) INFORMATION BOARD, with the **Area Ermita Vella** behind (*P*3).

    Turn left; the crags of Oltá's southern summit now rise steeply above you, as you climb gradually for about 100m/yds. After a sweeping right-hand bend, take the

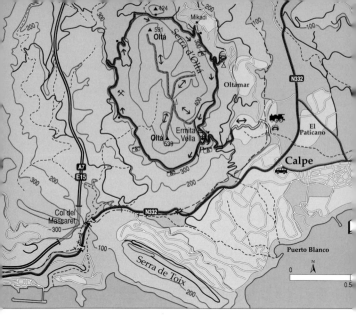

next track to the left, signposted 'Olta Sur'. *(But for the Alternative walk, fork right here.)* You are now on level ground again, and Calpe is spread out before you, from its southern harbour under the Morro de Toix to the Penyal d'Ifach guarding its northern harbour.

Reach a large open area on the left (**40min**) and two minutes later, ignore a track going left. As you continue, the panorama now includes the Mascarat Gorge with its three tunnels overlooked by the ruins of Calpe Castle. Beyond the castle, the Serra Gelada shelters Benidorm from the sea. The track undulates as it contours around the southwestern flank of Oltá.

Throughout the traverse of this western flank the peaks of the Serra Bernia dominate the skyline to the west, more of it coming into view with every step you take. Watch as the whole length of this magnificent ridge, shown opposite, opens out before you. Pass a RUINED HOUSE perched on the hillside (**1h**), then ignore a track coming in from the left. Continue past an old gabbro QUARRY, evidenced by the grey rocks strewn around. Ignore another track coming in from the left at the quarry, but take note of the 'needles' below Oltá's north summit and another abandoned house. At a T-junction (**1h14min**) turn sharp right to reach the HOUSE (**1h23min**), from where the photograph opposite was taken.

Now, as you climb steeply, Oltá's northern summit (591m/1940ft) towers above you. Pass below the 'needles' and an interesting rock formation, ignoring firebreak tracks off to the right. The track descends to meet another track at a T-junction (**1h34min**). Turn right here and head for yet another RUINED HOUSE situated between the north summit and Little Oltá (424m/1390ft). The flat area in front of the house is a good place to take a break.

As you continue, the track narrows to a path and begins descending, first gradually, then ever more steeply. Watch for the waymarks on this descent. The surrounding area is covered in low scrub and fallen trees. Join a forestry track (**1h50min**) and turn right. The track sweeps round to join an asphalt road at CASA MIKADI (**1h57min**), where you turn right. Some 100m/yds further on the road sweeps to the left past another villa; here keep straight ahead on a mainly level track. Shortly after it narrows, bear right at a junction and go up a short rocky waymarked section. Then wind through pines, often alive with the twittering of coal tits and long tailed tits. You enjoy glimpses of the coast, from the Cap de Moraira to Calpe, with the Penyal d'Ifach and Calpe Salinas domin-ating the scene (photograph page 19). At a junction (**2h10min**), turn right on a forestry road. *(Motorists using the alternative starting point come in from the left and go back the same way at this junction.)* Ignore tracks off to houses or beckoning you up the mountain.

Soon the southern summit of Oltá (539m/1968ft) appears ahead of you. At the junction (**2h30min**) your circuit is complete: turn left, retracing your outward route back to **Calpe** STATION (**3h20min**). *(But those starting out from the campsite should continue on the circuit track.)*

Bernia Ridge, from the house passed at 1h23min into the walk

4 THE FOUR FACES OF PUIG CAMPANA

See photograph page 136   **Distance**: 12km/7.5mi; 3h39min

Grade: Strenuous, with an ascent/descent of 570m/1870ft; well way-marked PR 289 throughout (yellow/white flashes)

Equipment: see page 42

How to get there and return: 🚗 car to the 6km-point in Car tour 4: instead of turning left to Sella, turn right into Finestrat. At the main crossroads in the town centre, turn left (signed 'Font del Molí') and drive 1km to the *font*. Park just beyond the *font* on the right. 🚌 to the crossroads in the centre of Finestrat. Walk up the hill to Font del Molí (25 min). Return bus times are variable — ask your driver. If necessary get a taxi or walk back and catch a bus at Carrefour/La Marina.

Short walk: Font del Molí — lower slopes. 6km/3.8mi; 1h43min. Easy, with one short ascent/descent of 150m/500ft. Start as for the main walk and turn right on the track at the 1min-point. Follow the yellow and white PR waymarks (this is the end of main walk, but in reverse), taking care not to miss the path off right in 13min. Meet a track at a signpost and turn right (35min) but, after just 200m/yds (on the first bend), turn left on a track and immediately left again on a cairned path. Descend gradually through old terraces and pine woods, cross a *barranco* and meet a wider path waymarked in red (53min). Turn sharp right. Cross the barranco again and then go straight across a track (1h08min). When you meet a track by a ruined house (1h19min), turn right, then turn right again on a road. Within 200m/yds pass a road on the left.* About 10m/yds further on, take the road going left and snaking round the hillside, above a reservoir, back to Font del Molí (1h43min).

*This is the direct route back to Finestrat (also 1h43min). The road becomes a path after 50m/yds, as it passes Villa San Miguel.

Each of the four faces of Campana has its own mood and its own distinctive vegetation. With views changing spectacularly as you move around the mountain, you will find this a most satisfying walk.

    Start out at **Font del Molí**: continue up the asphalt road (immediately ignoring a wider road to the right). You pass a track to the right (**1min**); this is your return route. Just after crossing a bridge over a water channel (**11min**), take the wide track uphill to the right. After 30m/yds you come to a signpost for the PR 289 (yellow/white waymarks). Follow this to the left, ignoring the path signposted straight ahead to the summit of Campana. Soon you enjoy views to Aitana, Penya Sella and the 'sharks' teeth' of Castellets to the left and the west face of Campana rising steeply to the right. You climb through slopes covered in rosemary and bell heather in an area known as the **Roc de Bardalet** (**50min**) with spectacular views.

    Still climbing quite steadily, you'll soon round the bend to the north side of the mountain, where the cooler slopes are coloured with the blue, purple and yellow of rosemary, heather and gorse. As you round a bend (**1h 09min**), notice a *finca* (Mas de l'Oficial) below and the cliffs of Ponoch ahead to the left. Climb to the right of a metal MOUNTAINEERS' HUT (**1h34min**); the path broadens as it rises to the **Collado del Pouet** (**1h46min**), an open grassy area with a large flat rock — a good spot for a rest.

Five paths meet at this pass. Your incoming path continues slightly downhill. Another path comes up from the Mas de l'Oficial. A PR-marked path goes left towards the cliffs below Ponoch, eventually leading to Polop. And finally, to the right, your onward track goes uphill. Follow it up and, as it turns right, follow the PR 389 path going left (**1h50min**), now contouring round towards the eastern face of Campana. As the Serra Gelada comes into view, the path drops to run below a sheer cliff. Always clear, the path continues under the softer eastern face of Campana. At first you pass through low scrub but later through rock and scree, always contouring at around 900m and ignoring all climbers' paths up the mountain.

The south face comes into view (**2h24min**) as you head around a *barranco* descending from the summit. Cross a flat open area and soon begin a steady descent, heading towards the western end of the Cortina Ridge. Roldan's Notch is clearly visible on your right as the path steepens and zigzags to ease the descent over the rocks. When you reach an obvious junction of paths on a level stretch in amongst pine trees (**2h49min**), fork right. This quite wide path crosses a *barranco*, runs through a pine wood and eventually passes some old TERRACES and a ruined *casita* (**3h01min**).

You cross a track at a signpost (**3h 04min**; *the Short walk comes in here*) and soon begin a longish descent on a sometimes stony or rocky path. The path meets a track which you follow to a T-junction (**3h 31min**): go left, cross a deep water channel and, a couple of minutes later go left down the road, back to **Font del Moli** (**3h39min**).

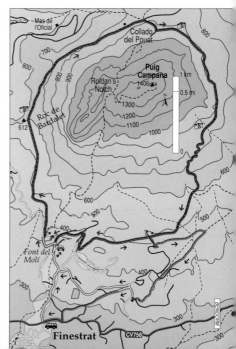

5 SERRA GELADA: FROM BENIDORM TO ALBIR

Distance: 10km/6.2mi; 4h   **See also town plan page 8**

Grade: strenuous, with steep ascents and corresponding descents of 625m/2050ft overall. You must be surefooted and have a head for heights. Paths are often eroded and sometimes uncomfortably close to the edge of the sheer cliffs (**danger of vertigo**). Navigation is straightforward, with good yellow/white PR waymarking past El Mendivil.

Equipment: see page 42; also proper walking boots or shoes, compass, extra water in summer

How to get there: 🚗 taxi, car or on foot to Calle de Hamburgo at the eastern end of Benidorm's Playa Levante — on the bend just as the road rounds the headland at Punta de Pinet. Parking could be difficult in the summer months.

To return: 🚐 from l'Albir; alight at Rincón de l'Oix (if you parked your car at Punta de Pinet) or in the centre of Benidorm.

Short walks (access as main walk; equipment as page 42)

1 Benidorm — El Mendivil — Benidorm. 4km/2.5mi; 1h50min. Fairly strenuous climb/descent of 330m/1080ft, but no danger of vertigo. Follow the main walk for 56min, then return the same way.

2 Benidorm — La Torre — Benidorm. 3km/1.9mi; 1h15min. Easy. Go through the gap in the blue railings at Playa Levante ('Entrada a la Playa' is painted on the rocks), and head down to the cove below. Take the path round to the headland above the next cove, Cala Ti Ximo. From here follow an asphalt road to the next headland, then continue on a footpath to the Punta de la Escaleta (**P**5). Now climb a path up to another asphalt road and follow it to the ruins of La Torre, a 17th-century watchtower (35min) with a superb outlook to the cliffs of the Serra Gelada. To return, either retrace your steps or follow the asphalt road.

Despite its proximity to Benidorm, the Serra Gelada is no mean mountain and must be treated with respect. From the landward side its undulating silhouette appears benign, but from the sea its sheer, stepped cliffs present a formidable picture. This exhilarating hike follows the cliff edge, with fantastic views.

The Serra Gelada, from the top of the first gully. Five major gullies are crossed before reaching the relay station on the highest point in the range (438m/1440ft).

Start out by walking up CALLE DE HAMBURGO, over-looking the **Playa Levante** and small cove. When the BLUE RAILINGS end, continue up to the left. Turn left past the CASTELL DEL MAR APARTMENTS (**4min**), then turn right up the hill (**8min**). Ignore a road off left after a few metres/yards. Rounding a bend, notice the hill to the left of the Radio Benidorm antennas — your first objective. It bears a metal cross. A steep, eroded short-cut path goes up to the left (**23min**), but we continue along the road. Pass the ANTENNAS (**28min**) and, just before coming level with the summit, take the path up right to the SUMMIT (**31min**), then catch your breath while enjoying the views.

From here progress along the ridge, heading generally northeast, alternately climbing to the cliff tops and then dropping steeply to cross the gullies. Either take the narrow path going down to the right just past the cross, or continue on the main path; the two paths rejoin a few metres below. Descend to a fork and bear left above a *barranco* on a well-trodden rocky path. It takes you round the head of the *barranco* (**38min**) and starts climbing to the top of the first cliff. This spot, popular with retired expatriates and locals alike, is marked with a small cairn (**El Mendivil**; 338m/1100ft; **56min**). *Short walk 1 turns back here.*

From here the walk, well way-marked with yellow and white flashes, makes for the end of the serra, where the antenna of the relay station is visible. But there are a lot of ups and downs to negotiate before you reach it. From the myriad of

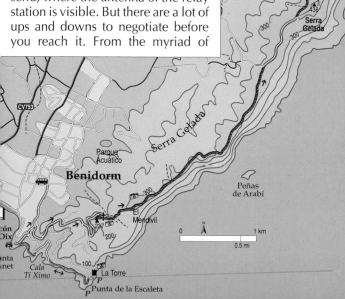

small paths round the cairn, take the most obvious one along the cliff top (the ONLY WAYMARKED ROUTE). When you come to the end of the level section, take the rough, rocky waymarked path; it descends into a gully, close to the edge of the cliff. Cross the gully (**1h08min**) and, having lost about 50m/165ft of altitude, you must now regain it. Continue within a few metres/yards of the cliff edge to the next peak. Cairns supplement the waymarks as you head down into the next, shallower gully. As you cross it (**1h25min**), you can see two routes up to the next peak. Make your choice of path and reach the top at **1h31min**. Below and ahead of you is the little island, Peñas de Arabí, dwarfed by the towering cliffs of the Serra Gelada.

The path, clear but steep, and only about 10m/yds from the cliff edge, zigzags down into the next gully, before rising past the ruins of what was probably an ANIMAL PEN (**2h**). After crossing the small hump by the ruins, it descends to cross another gully. From here a steep climb (sometimes on all fours!) brings you to the penultimate peak (**2h30min**), from where you can see the asphalt road to the relay station. Now the path descends into the last gully, moves away from the cliffs, and joins the road (**2h40min**). Turn right and follow the road steeply uphill.

The surrounds of the relay station at the SUMMIT of the **Serra Gelada** (**3h**) are closed, and you descend about 50m/yds below its gates. Watch for your descent path, on the left. It is fairly clear and, once on it, you will see WAYMARKING, sometimes supplemented by ARROWS. The resort and beach at l'Albir lie far below, and the path heads in that general direction, initially contouring below the relay station. It passes under electricity cables and begins to descend steeply. Ignore short-cuts as it zigzags down, following the line of the cables. When the path forks (**3h10min**), go right through a pine wood. After an open, fairly level section, the path splits again (**3h20min**): take either fork — they meet up again about five minutes later.

Eventually you wind down to a FIVE-WAY JUNCTION (**3h35min**), at a flattish piece of ground level with apart-ments on the left. Go right and keep following the cables, ignoring all crossing paths. You can see the road to the l'Albir lighthouse passing through a tunnel below. When you reach this road (CAMI VELL DEL FAR; **3h45min**), follow it to the left as it winds towards l'Albir's promenade. Cross the main road by the cafés and bars in **l'Albir**, and turn right for about 100m/yds, to the BUS STOP (**4h**).

6 SERPIS GORGE

Distance: 20km/12.4mi; 5h   **See also photographs pages 26, 63**

Grade: easy, level, out-and-back walk along the route of an old railway line. Fairly long, with some tunnels. Yellow/white PR waymarking.

Equipment: see page 42; *plus torch*

How to get there and return: 🚌 to L'Orxa (the 72km-point on Car tour 2). Just before the bridge over the Serpis River, on the western outskirts of the village, turn left uphill and park at the old station.

Short walk: Castell de Perputxent. 1km/0.6mi; 40min. Easy. Equipment as page 42; access as main walk. Climb the steep rocky path about 30m/yds to the right of L'Orxa station to the castle shown on pages 26 and 63 (20min). A gap by one of its two towers provides entry.

Alternative walks

1 Serpis circuit: 15km/9.3mi; 4h10min. Strenuous ascent/descent of 350m/1150ft. Equipment, access as main walk. Follow the main walk to the 1h38min-point, then take the signposted path to the right. It winds steeply up through abandoned terraces and past a waterfall. Pass well to the left of a house (2h05min), still climbing steeply. At a surfaced track, turn right. Keep to the asphalt past several houses but, just after two houses on the left, turn sharp right at a junction (signposted to L'Orxa). Then, at a large ornate house, turn right again. Climb steeply to an open area on a crest (2h35min), where a signposted path goes up

Second dam on the Serpis (1h38min)

left to the summit of Safor. Keep straight ahead here, using the map to follow Walk 7 (in reverse) down to L'Orxa (4h). At the CV701, turn right, back to your car.

2 Longer Serpis circuit. 22km/13.6mi; about 6h. Strenuous. Follow the main walk to the 2h30min-point, then return to the fork and go left. Use the map to rise up to the surfaced track below Safor and follow Walk 7 (in reverse) down to L'Orxa. At the CV701, turn right, back to your car.

This pleasant riverside stroll through the picturesque Serpis Gorge can be enjoyed by anyone. From the level track you can appreciate the marked contrast between the sheer cliffs surrounding the gorge and the gentleness of the river flowing through it. The river valley provides an ideal habitat for wild flowers and birds; allow a full day for picnicking, botanising and birdwatching.

Start the walk from **L'Orxa** STATION by following the old railway line below the castle. Just after a bend, alongside a little RUINED HOUSE (**9min**), ignore a track off to the right (**P**6a); continue through extensive olive terraces to the FIRST OF THE TUNNELS (**30min**). This is quite long, but soon after entering you can see the other end.

You emerge in a gentle landscape with low trees and, in spring, wild flowers everywhere. The heavily-reeded river banks are alive with the song of Cetti's warblers in spring and summer, and crag martins swoop hither and thither as they catch their food on the wing. Fish, some of them unbelievably large, swim unconcernedly in the clear water, and grey herons feed well.

At **46min** a path goes off right to a dam (**P**6b) — the source of the *canaleta* that runs along to the rather grand old hydroelectric station on the opposite side of the river (as you approach it, you will see and hear water cascading down a channel from the *canaleta* above). Leave the track at **1h14min**: go down towards the river and cross it on a low BRIDGE. Just past the chained entrance to the HYDRO-ELECTRIC STATION (now a water quality control station), take a small path up to a pretty, ruined *ermita*.

Continue along the track, the river now on your left. You rejoin the railway line at an old ruined BRIDGE (**1h23min**), where it used to cross the river. Lush orange groves lie between you and the river, before you go through a very short TUNNEL (**1h28min**). After two houses, and just

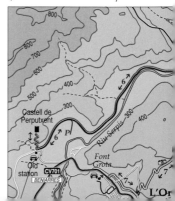

opposite the dam shown on page 59, note a walkers' signpost indicating a steep path up to the right (**1h38min**; *route of Alternative walk 1*). Continue straight ahead here, through the next TUNNEL (**1h41min**) — not much more than a wide arch. Soon you will reach a BRIDGE over an open grassy area (**1h49min**) with paths down to the river — an obvious spot to take a break.

Then continue along the track and through a cutting. There are more orange groves down by the river and another *canaleta* runs along the opposite bank. Negotiate another, fairly long TUNNEL (**1h55min**). The LAST OF THE TUNNELS (**2h05min**) is the longest (500m/0.3mi), but can be avoided: just before the entrance, scramble a couple of metres/yards down the slope to the left, then walk along a narrow path to the far end. You will pass a ruined building, probably an OLD MILL, on the river bank before rejoining the railway line (**2h14min**).

When you come to a fork, keep left *(Alternative walk 2 turns left here on the return)*. Now high above the river, follow the railway through pine woods, until you come to the end of the line — another dismantled BRIDGE (**2h30min**). Standing on top of the old supports, you have a glorious panoramic view of the amphitheatre created by the high, rugged peaks and sheer cliffs of Safor. Retrace your steps from here to **L'Orxa** STATION (**5h**).

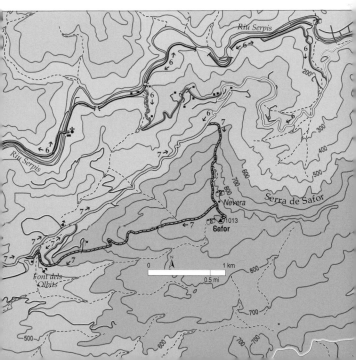

7 SERRA DE SAFOR

See map pages 60-61   Distance: 13km/8mi; 5h20min

Grade: fairly strenuous, with an ascent and corresponding descent of 765m/2500ft. Paths are good and navigation straightforward; well waymarked with yellow/white PR flashes..

Equipment: see page 42; also compass and long trousers

How to get there and return: ⊟ to L'Orxa (the 72km-point on Car tour 2). Shortly after crossing the Serpis River, on the western outskirts of the village, park on the right at the Font Grota — alongside a small garden with stone tables.

Short walk: L'Orxa — Font dels Olbits — L'Orxa. 7km/4.3mi; 2h20min. Easy climb and descent of 290m/950ft. Equipment as page 42; access as main walk. Follow the main walk past the 1h-point, then take the track on the right to the Font dels Olbits. Return the same way.

Approaching from the west, Safor looks fairly gentle but, from the north, its jagged peaks and sheer cliffs present quite a different spectacle. Its ascent offers a variety of experiences and scenery. Just below the summit there is a *nevera* and, on the way down, you can take a relaxing break at the picturesque Font dels Olbits.

Start out at the **Font Grota**: cross the road and turn right on the track which runs along the far side of the wide old river bed, now concreted. Pass two small footbridges; after the second, turn left for 65m/yds, then walk 10m/yds up towards the entrance to a house. Just before the house, turn right up a zigzag footpath. When you reach a narrow asphalt road (**6min**) turn right. You will now follow this winding road uphill for more than an hour, so relax and enjoy the scenery as it unfolds around successive bends. In **15min**, looking back to the southwest, you enjoy the view shown below. After a while the road levels out (**24min**) and skirts above the **Barranc del Bassiete**. About 10 minutes later, down to the left, you have a brief view of the Serpis Gorge (Walk 6). After passing some large almond terraces at the head of the *barranco*, the Font dels Olbits becomes visible ahead, set into the lower slopes of Safor (**46min**). At this point ignore a signposted track to the right.

As the road passes between patches of well-cultivated land, watch for a huge galvanised iron WATER TANK on the

After 15 minutes' climbing, look back over L'Orxa against the backdrop of Montcabrer. Benicadell rises to the right.

left (**1h**). About 200m/yds further on, a track to the right leads to the Font dels Olbits. We visit it on the return from Safor, *but the Short walk turns right here.* Continue along the road. Ignore a track to the right and, later, a concreted track going down into the valley to the left (**1h15min**).

You come to an open area on the left (**1h35min**; *Alternative walk 6-1 comes in here*). The steep, signposted path to 'SIM DE LA SAFOR' heads up the ridge to your right. It is well-trodden, but you will find long trousers handy if the lacerating scrub has not been cut back. As you ascend, take careful note when you reach some CRAGS (**1h50min**) that your path splits into two. Both forks go to the same place; we prefer the right-hand path. The paths rejoin (**2h20min**) and, shortly afterwards, you enjoy a magnificent view of the broad amphitheatre formed by the northern face of Safor. Nearby, the 'eye of the needle' — a natural rock arch — frames another view, down over the coastal plain.

Continue the ascent and reach a flat grassy 'MEADOW' just below the summit (**2h50min**). Here you can investigate the remains of an underground *nevera* (snow well), before the final, 10-minute ascent up the obvious path to the cross and TRIG POINT on **Safor** (1013m/3325ft; **3h**). From this summit much of the Costa Blanca is visible below. Ahead, the *huerta* spreads out its blanket of cultivation. To the northeast lies Gandía and the high-rise developments of the *playas;* the River Serpis (Walk 6) flows in the north. The western skyline is pierced by the distinctive peak of Benicadell. The reservoir at Beniarrés glimmers in the southwest, while the Vall de Gallinera spreads across the southern front, with the massed ranks of the serras of Alicante beyond it. Finally, Montgó (Walk 1) rises to the southeast, with Dénia and Xábia at its feet.

Retrace your steps to the meadow and take care here to locate the correct path for the descent. Go along the meadow to the left (southwest). The main path at the end of the meadow goes straight ahead, but leads only into difficult terrain with some very deep potholes. Your path

While at L'Orxa visit the old station (where Walk 6 begins) and the Castell de Perputxtent above it.

goes to the right just before entering the trees — be sure to find the clear YELLOW AND WHITE WAYMARKS. From this point, the route down is clear. Follow the waymarked path, fairly level at first, but gradually getting steeper as it descends. At **3h55min** note a walkers' signpost and a track to the right — a short cut back to your outward route. But take the path ahead to the **Font dels Olbits** (**4h05min**).

Beyond the *font,* you have two options. You can take the track leading round the benches, to rejoin your outward track near the large iron water tank, and turn left. Alternatively, as you head away from the *font,* locate some steps on the left, with PR waymarks. They lead to a narrow path which winds downhill and crosses the *barranco,* to the *finca* on the opposite side. From the *finca* a track leads to the track you followed on the outward route. Whichever option you take, on reaching your outgoing route, turn left back down to **L'Orxa** (**5h20min**).

View from the Font dels Olbits. The area around the font (which has a year-round water supply), has been beautifully restored, with benches and tables from where you can enjoy this magnificent landscape. Terraces, now largely unexploited, cover the low hills, while Benica-dell, sometimes likened to the Matterhorn, rises in the distance.

8 PONT DE LES CALDERES • BARRANCO DE LA ENCANTADA • ERMITA DE SANTO CRISTO • PONT DE LES CALDERES

Distance: 10km/6.2mi; 2h55min

Grade: moderate, but the climb up to the *ermita* (140m/460ft) is quite strenuous. Paths and tracks are good; navigation is straightforward.

Equipment: see page 42

How to get there and return: 🚌 to/from the Pont de les Calderes, at the 29km marker on the CV700 between Muro and Pego (the 53km-point on Car tour 2). Park well off the road, just to the west of the bridge, opposite the road down to the Barranco de la Encantada (with a sign, 'Camí de l'Almadec').

Short walk: Barranco de la Encantada. 4km/2.5mi; 1h16min. Easy. Equipment and access as above. Follow the main walk to the mill (38min) and return the same way.

Alternative return: At the 2h11min-point turn left on the metalled road, to the modern white house on the saddle. Then take a path off left 100m/yds before the house, back down to your outgoing route near Villa Mónica — or continue ahead to rejoin the main walk (see map).

In addition to exceptional views, this delightful walk offers a peaceful stroll by a stream, deep pools under the imposing cliffs of an impressive gorge, an optional detour to Planes with its ancient aqueduct and Moorish castle, and an old pilgrimage trail to an *ermita*. Autumn, when the heather is purple on the hillsides and trees in the valleys shine yellow and gold, is the best time of year.

Begin the walk at the **Pont de les Calderes**: follow the signposted road to the **Barranco de la Encantada**; it is asphalted at first, but not in good condition. Descending slightly through orchards, it leads to a ruined *casita* (**10min**) and your first glimpse of water in the *barranco* on the right. A little further on, you pass a ford across the watercourse, and the cliffs of the gorge begin to appear. The sound of running water accompanies you, as the gorge becomes deeper. In **15min** wooden steps beckon you down to the first of the pools, but only a minute ahead are the steps to the main POOLS (**P**8a). Calcium salts give the water a green and cloudy look, but it is fresh and cool.

Continue along what is now a track and, as you leave this narrow section of gorge, terracing opens out around you. The Serra de la Albureca appears ahead, while to the right are the rugged crags of the Serra de Foradá. At **24min** the track forks to the left of a newish white house and about a minute later peters out into a path, as it passes the black gates of VILLA MONICA. Descending through a small orchard, the path leads you beside a stream running through small green fields. Ignore a path going uphill to the left as your path goes along the edge of a ploughed

65

From the heights above the Barranco de la Encantada, there is a magnificent view of the church at Beniarrés, standing proud above the village. The Serra de Benicadell fills in the background.

field. You come upon pools, a tiny RESERVOIR (**P**8b) and another ruined *casita* (**31min**). More rugged peaks are visible ahead as the gorge closes in.

This is a popular walk so several paths have been created. As long as you keep the *barranco* on your right, you can take whichever you wish — they all lead to the same place — 'an old MILL by the stream' (**38min**). The *barranco* becomes very deep and sheer at this point. *The Short walk turns back here.* The path climbs up to the left then levels out near the top of the cliff, with views down the remainder of the *barranco* to the Serpis River (**51min**).

Continue upwards through olive terraces to a small building. Walk past the gate at the right of the building (the fruit on the trees just below the gate, bright orange when ripe, is *kaki* — persimmon). Continue through the remainder of the terraces and turn left on the surfaced road you meet at the ridge (**1h01min**). But first spend a few minutes taking in the fantastic views below — the upper Serpis Valley, the Embalse de Beniarrés, and the magnificent Serra de Benicadell almost straight ahead. Walk down the road in the setting shown above; VILLA ISABELITA (**1h09min**) commands the sort of views that most of us can only dream about.

At **1h33min** the village of Planes comes into view.* As

*You can make a (highly recommended) detour into Planes at the 1h38min-point: pass the steps and continue down the road for 200m/yds, then take the road to the right. Cross the barranco and keep uphill to the font (still in use) and the aqueduct (10min). From here you can easily see your way through the village to the Moorish castle (10min). After the detour return to the steps to continue.

you meet the asphalt road, turn left; after about 200m/yds (just past the 1km marker), take STEPS up left (**1h38min**) towards the Ermita de Santo Cristo. The first few steps are concrete, but the rest are hewn out of natural rock and make for an easy, though strenuous, ascent. Take it slowly, admire the views and count the STATIONS OF THE CROSS as you go. The twelfth station appears at **2h**, as you meet the road which winds round the back of the hill from Planes. There is a thirteenth station just before the entrance to the **Ermita de Santo Cristo** (**2h01min**), where you will also find picnic benches and fantastic views.

Leave the *ermita* by heading downhill on the asphalt road. The Embalse de Beniarrés sparkles below and, if you are lucky, you may see Bonelli's eagles soaring above. They are resident in this area of Spain, and their white bodies and darker wings make them identifiable with the naked eye. At the crossroads (**2h11min**) go straight ahead on a narrow track *(but left for the Alternative return)*,, walking through mixed fruit orchards down into and across a *barranco*. Ignore all tracks going off into terraces, but soon after the *barranco* take the left fork (the right fork goes up to a visible gatepost). Zigzag quite sharply uphill.

At **2h26min** a modern white house comes into view on the saddle, and you meet another fork. This time take the track which climbs to the right. When it levels out, you can almost see down the Barranco de la Encantada again (behind a house on the left). A minute later, as you meet another track (**2h36min**), turn right. This track descends along a heather-clad ridge, with the Barranco de la Encantada on the left and views over to the *ermita* and Planes on your right, providing a wonderful overview of the countryside traversed throughout the walk. The track takes you all the way back to the **Pont de les Calderes** (**2h55min**).

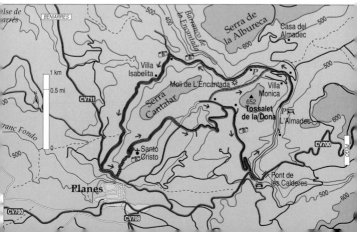

9 L'ATZUBIA • CASTELL DE GALLINERA • ALMISERA • L'ATZUBIA

Distance: 11km/6.8mi; 3h20min

Grade: fairly strenuous, with prolonged, sometimes steep, ascents and corresponding descents of 540m/1770ft. Tracks and paths are good; navigation is straightforward.

Equipment: see page 42

How to get there and return: ⛟ to L'Atzubia (Adsubia) on the CV700 5km west of Pego (the 97km-point on Car tour 2); park in the tiny square.

Short walks: Gallinera Castle. Fairly strenuous ascent/descent of 300m/ 980ft. Equipment, access as main walk. Follow the main walk to the first saddle and back (fine view of the castle; 5.5km/3.4mi; 1h45min) or go to the saddle below the castle and back (7km/4.3mi; 2h15min).

Alternative walk: L'Atzubia — Castell de Gallinera — Almiserá — L'Atzubia. 10km/6.2mi; 2h45min. Equipment, access and grade as main walk, but you must also be surefooted and have a head for heights. This walk covers the same ground as the main walk, but instead of skirting below the Almiserá cliffs on the track, it follows a narrow footpath (**danger of vertigo**). Follow the main walk to the track by Gallinera Castle (1h06min), where the main walk turns left. Here take a PR-waymarked path between the track and your outward path. This narrow and rocky path, clearly marked, leads under the northern cliffs of Almiserá. It crosses a few short scree runs horizontally, and leads to some beehives after about 30min. At the beehives, turn right on a track. On reaching an asphalt road, turn left and pick up the main walk at the 2h14min-point (notes on page 72).

This walk takes you through rural countryside, ascends an old mule trail, contours under imposing cliffs, and offers unbelievable views of one of the region's strategically-sited castles. Birdwatchers and botanists will find much to interest them in this varied terrain.

The walk starts in the tiny MAIN SQUARE in **L'Atzubia**, by the *font* just outside the unmistakeable bar-disco L'EIXAM. Climb the road by the *font* (CALLE PRINCIPAL) all the way past the CHURCH. When you reach the steps by the cross, take the middle road, which bears slightly left. Despite being surfaced, this road sees little traffic. It takes you through the orange groves at the beginnings of the very fertile Gallinera Valley and alongside the Barranco de Michel down to your left. All the time you will be climbing steadily, so take it slowly and enjoy the pleasant country atmosphere. Ahead you can see the Castell de Gallinera and higher up, to its left, the TV antennas on top of Almiserá. Even further to the left, your return route is visible, snaking down the hillside. Ignore a road off to the left (**10min**) and start climbing a little more steeply.

At **18min**, as you go under the electricity lines, make sure to follow the road round a hairpin to the left, ignoring the track going straight ahead. Many of the terraces

On the approach to Gallinera Castle, 1h into the walk. You can take a 20min return detour to the castle, but it is privately owned and kept locked.

around here are cultivated with *algarrobas* — carob or locust beans; they are used for animal feed. Nowadays, however, this crop is less popular and rarely seen. The road zigzags up towards an obvious saddle below Almiserá, and you will have passed a few houses by the time it becomes a track (**29min**). It then winds steadily up the lower slopes of Almiserá, its antennas still visible above. The orange groves have been left far below; only carobs, olives and almonds grace these higher slopes.

You will probably already have noticed the little white *casita* clinging to the slopes above you to the left — you will pass this shortly. Looking back as you contour along one of the flatter sections, there is a good view of L'Atzubia, framed in the hills, with the coastal plain and the sea behind it. At a junction (**35min**) go uphill to the right. Just before reaching the power lines again, turn right on the track marked with a RED ARROW (**43min**). Ignore a track coming in from the left, and pass in front of the white *casita* (**46min**). Continue straight ahead on what is now just an old narrow mule trail which zigzags up over the terraces. Follow the red markers, ignoring a path coming in from the left just before reaching the SADDLE (**53min**), from where there is a superb view of Gallinera Castle. *The first Short walk option turns back here.*

From the saddle you can pick out the next part of your route going round the slopes towards the castle. The well-marked path is level at first, then it climbs through some old almond terraces. You pass to the left of a ruined *casita,* before levelling out a bit under a crag and joining a track on another SADDLE just below the **Castell de Gallinera** (**1h06min**); see photograph above. (This track goes all the way down into the valley, to the village of Benirrama, which claims the castle as its own and calls it Castell de Benirrama.) *The second Short walk turns back here.*

Turn left on the track, to circle under the imposing cliffs of **Almiserá**. *(The path here, lying between your upward route and the track you are now following, is the route of the Alternative walk.)* YELLOW AND WHITE PR

WAYMARKS replace the red markings and, as you set off on this new track, you have a magnificent view of the entire Gallinera Valley below to the right. The track is initially wide, but in very poor condition — rocky, or just stony, and deeply furrowed by running water; the presence of several large boulders indicates the instability of the cliffs above. As you proceed, the track deteriorates further — at times it is little more than a footpath. Your views of the castle, however, continue to improve!

Ignore paths off to the terraces and continue uphill beneath the cliffs, which are home to peregrine falcons and ravens. As you approach the plateau below Almiserá, the landscape opens out, heralding a change in bird life — look out for black redstart, goldfinch and wheatear. At **1h 45min** you are on the wide plateau which stretches between Vall de Gallinera and Vall d'Ebo and, if it is a Sunday or a *fiesta* in autumn, you may spot a number of *seta* (wild mushroom) gatherers foraging in the vegetation, baskets or buckets hanging hopefully over their arms.

At **1h53min** join a narrow surfaced road and turn left. At the top of the hill (**2h**) the energetic may like to turn left and climb up the road to the SUMMIT OF **Almiserá** (757m/

2480ft). But the main walk heads downhill to the right here, with Pego visible just beyond the valley below, and the coast clear in the distance. The crags of Almiserá loom starkly on the left as the road winds quite steeply down towards Pego. At **2h09min**, on a particularly sharp hairpin bend to the left, there is a small open area with a large boulder. A narrow path goes straight ahead and provides a fragrant short-cut which avoids that long bend. Rejoin the road five minutes later (**2h14min**); *the Alternative walk comes in here*. The rocky hillsides are carpeted with herbs, dwarf palms, gorse and heather, and you will pass several *casitas*.

At **2h23min** turn left on a narrow road (where there is a FIRE RISK WARNING SIGN). This is your road back into L'Atzubia. Follow it past some houses before reaching the top of a small rise, from where you have a view of L'Atzubia nestling in the valley below. It's a long way down, so the road zigzags steeply — very hard on the knees! It is in such a poor state of repair that we have never met any vehicles on it.

As you drop through the terraces there are wide views down the sheer slopes into the valley. At **3h** giant reeds line a small *barranco,* and the *algarrobas* and almonds give way to orange and cherry trees. The road crosses another *barranco* and takes you straight up a short steep rise, back to the *font* in **L'Atzubia** (**3h20min**).

10 SERRA DE LA CARRASCA AND THE MOZARABIC TRAILS

See map pages 70-71; see also photograph page 12

Distance: 23km/14.3mi; 6h50min

Grade: long and strenuous, with ascents and corresponding descents of 900m/2950ft. The first part of the walk is no longer maintained or way-marked; a couple of other stretches require careful navigation. *Only recommended in the cooler seasons.*

Equipment: see page 42; also *compass,* towel, picnic, plenty of water

How to get there and return: 🚌 to Fleix (the 122km-point on Car tour 1); park at the school, at the far (western) end of the village.

Short walk: Mozarabic trail. 2.5km/1.5mi; 1h10min. Easy descent/ strenuous re-ascent of 180m/590ft. Equipment, access as *Alternative walk 1.* Follow *Alternative walk 1* to the falls (30min) and return the same way.

Alternative walks

1 Embalse de Isbert. 5.5km/3.4mi; 2h40min. Strenuous descent/re-ascent of 260m/850ft. In summer, the bed of the Río Ebo can be a fur-nace; do *not* attempt this outside the cool season. Access and equipment as main walk (except compass). Follow the main walk to the *lavadero* (5min; *P*10b), then take the path down to the right 30m/yds further on — the beginning of the Mozarabic trail shown below. Descend through a rock arch (Forat) to the base of a (seasonal) waterfall (30min; *P*10c) and continue down to the pebbly river bed (45min; *P*10d). Turn right and wind downstream through this amazing gorge to the Embalse de Isbert (1h15min). Most of the year this reservoir is completely dry — hence its popular name, 'Isbert's Folly'. Return the same way.

2 Barranc del Infern and a Mozarabic trail. 10km/6.2mi; 3h. Strenuous, with ascents/descents of about 500m/1650ft. Park at the Font d'els Olbis on the CV721 west of Fleix. Follow the main walk from the 43min-point

The Mozarabic trail, seen from the rock arch (6h15min into the main walk, but only 25min from Fleix; Alternative walk 1 and Picnics 10c-d). The word Mozarabic ('would-be Arab') refers to Christians who were allowed to practise their religion under Moorish rule. To get around in the mountainous terrain they built narrow trails which cleverly stepped so that the usual difficulties associated with steep ascents and descents were minimised. Natural rock was used where possible, but for the most part they represent a remarkable feat of design and construction. Some have since fallen into disrepair and others have been lost to vegetation, some-times coming to light by chance or after a severe fire. But many remain in good order today and are a feature of several of the walks in this book.

to the 1h24min-point, then keep on the unmade road — to the abandoned houses of Juvees d'Alt (Upper Juvees). Just before a ruined house, at a signpost 'Font d'els Olbis', turn right on the yellow/white waymarked PR147. You descend via the Barranc del Tuerto to the Barranc de Racons, where Mozarabic steps come underfoot. Where a path comes in from the left, continue straight ahead for 'Benimaurell', back to the CV721, where you turn left to the Font d'els Olbis.

3 Barranc del Infern and Mozarabic trails via the PR147. 14.5km/9mi; 5h. Strenuous, with ascents/descents of about 900m/1950ft overall; access as main walk. Follow *Alternative walk 1* to the river bed, then continue up the far side on the PR147. When you meet an unmade road at the Pozo de la Juvea, follow it to a signpost 'Juvees d'Enmig' (Middle Juvees). Turn left here on a footpath. The path passes to the left of a house and runs downhill through terracing before coming to the Font del Réinos. Slither down to the river bed, where another sign directs you up to Juvees d'Alt (Upper Juvees). Turn right on the unmade road here for 200m/yds, passing a well on the right. Just past a ruined house on the left, the PR147 is signposted left to the Font d'els Olbis. You descend via the Barranc del Tuerto to the Barranc de Racons, where more Mozarabic steps come underfoot. Where a path comes in from the left, continue straight ahead for 'Benimaurell', back to the CV721, where you turn left past the Font d'els Olbis to Benimaurell. Keep to the CV721 past Bar Oasis, then take the unmade road forking left downhill. Follow this to back to Font Grossa and return to your car.

If you are fit enough to tackle a really long, full-day walk, then do not miss some version of this one. The main walk takes you along the Vall de Laguar, over the barren Carrasca Ridge and into Vall d'Ebo for a break in one of the bars. After crossing the Barranc del Infern, you return on a pair of Mozarabic trails, one plunging steeply down into the bed of the Ebo, the other thrusting back up again. But if you prefer not to walk cross-country without waymarks, the alternative walks are no less exhilarating.

Begin at the SCHOOL in **Fleix**: continue along the road past the school (YELLOW/WHITE PR WAYMARKS). Almost immediately, take the unmade road to the right. Pass **Font Grossa** and the village WASH-HOUSE shown on page 12 (**5min**; *P*10b). Some 30m/yds further on, the path down to the right is your return route (*turn down right here for Alternative walks 1 and 3 or* **P**10c, d). Continue winding gently up through almond groves, past another *font* and *lavadero*. Climb steeply into **Benimaurell** (**29min**); pass Bar Oasis and bear left to leave the village on the CV721. As you gain height, notice the Serra del Cavall Verd on the left, the Barranc del Infern on the right and the barren Carrasca Ridge ahead. After passing the **Font dels Olbis** on the right, with stone picnic tables and benches (**43min**), continue to the **Collado de la Garga** (**1h13min**). Turn right here, on an unmade road signposted

'Barranc del Infern', just at the right of the Venta el Collado restaurant. The main walk now bumbles its way to Carrasca, the ridge which looms ahead to your right. Ignore a track to the left (**1h18min**) and continue to an ANIMAL PEN below on a SADDLE (**1h24min**) at the head of two valleys: on the right, running northeast, is the Vall de Laguar; on the left, running southwest, is the beginning of the Jalón Valley. You will be heading, pathless, for the small saddle ahead, at the top of the Carrasca Ridge.

Some 50m/yds past the pen, go left off the track, making a beeline for saddle (350°). *(But for Alternative walk 2, keep ahead on the track.)* Sadly, this stretch is no longer waymarked, but you should reach the SADDLE at the top of **Carrasca Ridge** in about **2h05min**. Vall d'Ebo is far below, and you can see along the coast from Dénia to Gandía. The summit of Almiserá, with its TV antenna, is across the valley on the Gallinera Ridge.

On the same line of sight, but only about 20m/yds ahead of you, is the continuation of your route. You want to be contouring to the right about 20m/yds below the top of the ridge — heading northeast — up and round the left side of the rocky hillock about 500m/0.3mi away. So just make your way to the left slope of the hillock (**2h13min**), beyond which you see Almiserá and the TV antenna. From here walk down the wide flat ridge, heading west of north and keeping Almiserá ahead to the right. The village of Vall d'Ebo can be seen below, slightly to the right of the direction in which you are walking (**2h18min**). This spur will take you all the way down off the mountain.

The terrain makes for easy walking, but take care when the descent becomes a little steeper, with *barrancos* on either side. To the left of Vall d'Ebo village you'll see a *finca* with a red-tiled roof; in front of it there is a little stone shelter surrounded by extensive almond and olive terraces. Make your way down to the top TERRACE (**2h39min**), then circle left and downhill through the terraces to the SHELTER. From here, locate another small building on the opposite side of a *barranco* and contour round to it (**2h55min**). Pass just to the right of this building and continue round the groves, skirting to the left of a small hillock, until you reach a farm track just below. Turn right towards a *finca* and reach an asphalt road (**3h04min**). Follow it downhill to the right, into **Vall d'Ebo** (**3h20min**).

Refreshment is available in the village*, but if you have

*If you have been in the village centre, head east from Plaza Mayor until you reach the second (waymarked) bridge mentioned in the text.

a picnic, press on. Past the SPORTS CENTRE and CAMP GROUND, turn left to a BRIDGE OVER THE **Ebo** (**3h23min**). Don't cross it; turn right along the river. At the next BRIDGE, turn right, then sharp left (PR 43; YELLOW/WHITE WAYMARKS). Continue along the river, past the CEMETERY on your right (**3h33min**). A track takes you past a ford, to a junction (**3h39min**). If water is flowing, there is a good picnic spot by the river five minutes along the left fork (*P*10a). We head *right* here (signposted 'Vall de Laguar'), to **Font de Xili** (**3h44min**), another setting for *P*10a.

From Font de Xili the track continues high above the bed of the **Barranc del Infern**. Watch out on the left for the *clear, waymarked* PR 43 path down to the river bed (six minutes from the *font* at time of writing, but it may have been re-routed) — *be sure to locate the waymarks!* After crossing the river bed (**3h58min**), the path climbs for a few minutes, then begins to descend again. This section can be eroded in places. On reaching an ABAN-DONED ALMOND GROVE (**4h05min**) the path goes up to the right, climbing very steeply past a RUINED HOUSE. Turning sharp left after the house, the path continues rising through scrub to another almond grove and then a newer HOUSE (**4h20min**), where you may encounter dogs. Join the track leading from this house and meet an unmade road after a further 200m/yds. Turn right; the road takes you around the head of a *barranco*, past a crumbling house on the right, with a WELL (**4h38min**). Soon (**4h 44min**) you will spot several buildings on the far side of a little ravine — **Les Juvees d'Enmig** (Middle Juvees).

Follow the waymarks past this outpost and to the **Pozo de la Juvea** (**5h10min**), a well with five stone animal troughs. Walk round the well and descend the path to the left of the adjacent house, following a terrace wall. This is the beginning of your long zigzag descent into the bed of the Ebo on the MOZARABIC TRAIL shown on pages 72-73. After a while, look for the twin trail winding up the far side to your final destination, Fleix, and, part-way up, a waterfall — which must be imagined unless there has been heavy rain! Cross the (usually dry) bed of the **Ebo** (**5h55min**; *P*10d) and then zigzag up the far side, passing below the seasonal WATERFALL (**6h10min**) and under very steep cliffs (*P*10c). Go through a huge arch cut in the rock by the Mozarabs (**Forat**), pass across the top of the water-fall, and stagger up to the top (**6h44min**). Turn left to the *lavadero* and main road, then left again to the SCHOOL in **Fleix** (**6h50min**).

11 VUELTA DEL SOMO (SOMO CIRCUIT)

Distance: 11km/6.8mi; 3h19min

Grade: moderate, with ascents and corresponding descents of 260m/ 850ft. Good surfaces underfoot and straightforward navigation.

Equipment: see page 42

How to get there and return: 🚌 from Benidorm: take the CV715 north and turn left just past Tárbena, on the CV752. About 100m before the 3km marker (the 93km-point on Car tour 3), turn left on a road towards some houses (the Casas de Bixauca). Park at the point where the road sweeps left at a ruined house on the right.

For variety of terrain, overwhelming views and outstanding scenery, this walk comes near the top of the list. While Somo itself is an unremarkable mountain, as you make this anticlockwise circuit it becomes obvious why this is one of our favourite walks. Look out for golden eagles which hunt in the area … and for the tracks of the wild boar so prized by hunters.

Start out at the **Casas de Bixauca**: take the concrete track which goes off the bend to the right. You are making for the saddle to the west, where there is an orange building, and will then go around the back of Somo, the hill to its left, and return through the valley. Just at the far side of some ruins (**Finca Bixauca; 3min**), there is an open grassy area (**P**11a). But take a path a few metres/yards *before* the picnic spot, going downhill between drystone walls, to a track and a WELL (**6min**). Turn right and 100m/

Bolulla Castle rises on a ridge beyond almond groves, just 20min into the walk. To catch the almond trees in blossom, walk in early February. In April, cherry blossom will feature throughout this walk.

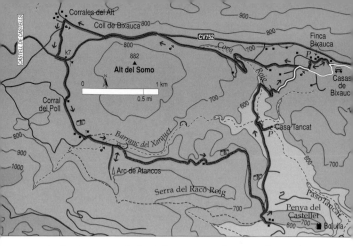

yds further on, fork right on another track (**9min**; your return route is the track on the left). Concreted in places, the track heads west through the almond groves shown on page 77, parallel with the CV752 road.

Ignore a track to the left and another to the right, then cross the **Barranc de la Cova Roig** (**24min**). The track, now almost a path, sweeps left and appears to be going in the wrong direction. But it is just gaining height and will soon zigzag round to the west again. At **40min** join a track which enters from the left and climbs gently past a galvanised WATER TANK to the road (**46min**). Turn left and climb to the saddle you saw earlier — the **Collao Bixauca** (**54min**), from where the peaks of Serrella rise ahead in the west. As you descend you'll see a track on the right, in the middle of a Z-bend (**1h**). Turn right on this track; it takes you on a gentle stroll through flat rural countryside. At a junction where there is a collection of houses (**Corrales del Alt; 1h09min**), turn left and head directly towards the craggy ridge of Aixorta. Fork left (**1h 11min**) past a WELL and reach the road again (**1h15min**). Watch out around here for corn buntings; their rattling call is unmistakable. Cross the road and take the wide track a few metres/yards to the left (just opposite the KM7 MARKER); head towards Aixorta. This is a popular spot for people gathering *setas* (wild mushrooms) in autumn.

The track, signposted 'Font dels Teixos', climbs gradually past a small pine wood and through almond groves to a house on the right (**1h31min**). Some 50m/yds further on, at a T-junction, go left (signposted 'Algibe Chorquet, PR151, ida y vuelta'). Ignoring a minor track off left to some ruins, follow the main track downhill into the beginnings of the **Barranc del Xarquet** (Barranco de Chorquet in Spanish). Off to the right, in a stony stream bed, is an ancient Moorish well, the **Aljibe Chorquet** (**1h35min**). (Just past the well, enthusiasts could take a 40min return detour: follow a track on the right. It leads to a point below a rock arch, the Arc de Atancos, from where it is possible to clamber up for a closer look.)

The main walk goes straight ahead here, following the Barranc del Xarquet. As the track sweeps downhill to the left, take a narrow path on the right (red waymark), edging an almond grove (**1h40min**). You will follow this narrow path for some time as it skirts around the **Serra del Racó Roig**, the Barranc del Xarquet deep on the left.

At **1h49min** a huge cave comes into view on the far side of the *barranco*. The path passes a stone shed and rounds some extensive but abandoned terraces (**2h**). Then you climb a rather desolate hillside to a CREST (**2h06min**), from where you enjoy a first good view of the sheer cliffs of **Paso Tancat** ('Closed Gorge'). Descending southwards, the views encompass the high peaks of the Bernia Ridge to the southeast, Bolulla Castle on its craggy ridge (Penya del Castellet) and the Serra Gelada to the south, close to Benidorm. Across the valley, to the left, you can see your homeward track snaking up to the houses around Finca Bixauca and, on the valley floor, a *finca* which you will reach later in the walk.

The path continues round the Serra del Racó Roig, all the while losing a little height (and crossing a rockfall), until it reaches a SADDLE (**2h30min**), where it meets a wide forestry track coming up from the valley. You will turn down left here, but first go over the saddle and look at the old settlement which locals call 'the high place'. One or two houses are being restored. From the saddle the crags below Bolulla Castle rise impressively above you.

Return to the track and descend it. Paso Tancat almost defies belief from this vantage point, so sheer are its cliffs. Ignore a track off right to terraces just before a short uphill section, and continue down to the valley floor. Soon after passing some olive groves a path goes right (**2h53min**) to **Casa Tancat**, the *finca* you saw from above. Surrounded by cherry groves, it is a perfect spot for a break (**P**11b).

From here the track climbs steeply out of the valley and eventually becomes asphalted. Looking back, you can marvel at the terrain you have just crossed. Just beyond some grassy terraces and a shed set amongst pines (**3h13min**), you reach the WELL passed on the outward route. Turn left up the path and then right on the concrete track, back to the **Casas de Bixauca** (**3h19min**).

12 FONTS DE L'ALGAR • SERRA DE BÉRNIA • BARRANC DE BINARREAL • FONTS DE L'ALGAR

See also photograph page 23

Distance: 20km/12.4mi; 6h

Grade: moderate-strenuous, with ascents and corresponding descents of 440m/1440ft. Good terrain underfoot. Navigation is straightforward. *After exceptionally heavy rains, the main walk and Alternative walk 2 will be impassable.*

Equipment: see page 42; also long trousers

How to get there and return: 🚗 to/from Casa Federico, Restaurante Bar La Cascada in Fonts de l'Algar (the 159km point on Car tour 1). NB: There are *no* buses.

Short walk: Algar Valley. 6km/3.7mi; 2h15min. Moderate climb/descent of 120m/395ft. Equipment as page 42. Access as main walk. Follow the main walk to the 32min-point. Go straight ahead on the quiet asphalt road which is basically level and gives good views all along the Algar Valley and Bernia Ridge. Walk to the end of the asphalt (56min) or the ruined houses (1h10min) and return the same way.

Alternative walks

1 Fonts de l'Algar — Serra de Bérnia — Fonts de l'Algar. 8.5km/5.2mi; 3h. Moderate-strenuous, with ascents and corresponding descents of 300m/980ft. Equipment as page 42; access as main walk. Follow the main walk to the 1h49min-point, then cross the valley and wind uphill to a T-junction where ahead there is a ruined house with outbuildings and about 50m/yds to the left a lovely well. Turn right and almost immediately left onto a track. You have rejoined the main walk at the 4h47min-point.

2 Circuit from Tárbena. 11km/6.8mi; 3h35min. Moderate; equipment as for main walk. Park at the *mirador* on the CV715 just below Restaurante Sa Cantarella (the 152km-point on Car tour 1). Walk a few metres uphill and cross over to take a surfaced track, PR waymarked, that climbs the bank and heads towards the Bernia Ridge. Follow the track to the 'stop' sign, go straight across, and pass to the right of the Nexo nightclub (9min). Pick up the main walk at the 3h57min-point and follow it to the junction at the 4h47min-point (59min). Carry on downhill, winding left. The track levels out and crosses the often-dry Algar River at the valley floor (1h17min). Leave the track as it bears right and take the rocky track off to the left, picking up the main walk after the 1h49min-point. Follow it to the 3h57min-point, where you turn right (3h25min), getting back to your car within ten minutes.

This walk takes you through two fertile valleys, where the varied countryside is quite gentle despite being surrounded by rugged and barren serras. A highlight is the impressive Pas dels Bandolers (Brigands' Pass). Birdwatchers and botanists will find much of interest, particularly in spring, and even if you don't actually see wild boar you will notice evidence of their presence.

Start out in the CAR PARK at **Casa Federico**. Go along by the water, past two small WATERFALLS (*P*12; photograph page 23) and into a narrow asphalt road with YELLOW AND

WHITE PR WAYMARKS. This road bears right (**3min**) and starts to climb very steeply. Ignore tracks to groves of oranges and *nísperos* (medlars) or houses and continue up to the TOP OF THE RISE (**21min**). From here the road is almost level. As you stop for a breather, look back to Campana, Ponoch, Aitana and Aixorta. Penya Severino (the end of the Serra de Bernia) and Ferrer rise to the right, their cliffs separated by a narrow vertical gap — the Pas dels Bandolers.

At a fork (**25min**) go right, heading directly towards Penya Severino and the Bernia Ridge. Walk through orange groves and pass a RESERVOIR just before a track goes off to the left — your return route (**32min**). The road takes you past avocado groves and steeply down to the valley floor, where you turn sharp left on a track (**40min**). Cross the river bed about a minute later and begin your ascent. You'll be on this clear track for some time, so just ignore tracks off to the groves and back to the river bed and concentrate on enjoying the spectacular scenery. There are good views of Campana and Ponoch through the cleft formed by the Algar. The track zigzags up then levels out and runs parallel to the Algar Valley. At a junction, where there is a large ruined *finca* on the left (**1h20min**), go straight ahead and slightly downhill on a track — towards another house, beautifully sited on a little spur (**1h33min**).

The track now winds down past abandoned houses (diggings of wild boar are particularly evident here) to the floor of the **Algar Valley** (**1h49min**). The main walk turns right here (first put on long trousers). *(But Alternative walk 1 goes left and crosses the valley.* You now follow the river bed all the way up the valley. *(If you need to use the stepping stones at the first crossing point, it undoubtedly means that completing the walk will be very difficult. We suggest you do Alternative walk 1 instead.)* The rocky track soon bends right, into the river bed, but you leave it after about three minutes, taking a narrow path which forks right and cuts off a bend in the river. Reach a CAIRN at the CONFLUENCE of the **Algar** and **Binarreal** (**1h58min**). Continue on the (sometimes overgrown) track which bears left up the narrow **Barranc de Binarreal**, a little-frequented valley. We have seen wild boar here ... and a golden eagle soaring above Ferrer. After heavy rain you might get your feet wet if there is water in the *barranco* bed. At **2h08min** pass the first *finca* up on the left, with well-kept terraces and carob trees. You'll now have to walk up the bed itself for a while. The track passes through pines before reaching an open area from where the awesome peaks of Ferrer rise on your right (**2h28min**).

Cross the open area and follow a rough track as it bears left, following the river bed. As the valley begins to open out, the Carrascal de Parcent fills in the background. Ignore a track coming in from the right (**2h 39min**) and carry on alongside a stream. The track climbs very steeply for a few minutes, past vegetable gardens on the right. When it becomes an asphalt road, continue upwards, but turn off left on a track heading into the valley (**2h48min**). When it forks four or five minutes later, go up to the right and wind around the terraces. Pass below covered orchards and a ruined house and proceed around the valley towards a SAND-COLOURED HOUSE. Reach the road again (**3h10min**) and turn left. Beyond the sand-coloured house (**3h14min**), as the road bends right (**3h18min**), take a concrete track off to the left and immediately fork left again on a surfaced track. Enjoy the views as it circles round the opposite side of the valley above orange groves. At about **3h27min** the track dips and asphalt gives way to dirt. Ignore tracks to the left and go up to the top of the rise (**3h32min**) which is on a right-hand bend. Pause here. You'll see two huge water tanks ahead, beneath the gap in the hills that you'll soon go through. Immediately over the rise there are two tracks to the right. Take the first of these, going uphill and passing behind a house. It is very steep and passes under another house on the right.

Meet a concreted track at a junction (**3h40min**) and turn up left. *Nísperos* and olive trees grace the terraces to the left, and the huge rocky outcrop of Cabaix towers over you to the right as you pass below it. On rounding a bend (**3h50min**) the NEXO NIGHT CLUB comes into view, and you reach it at a narrow road (**3h57min**). The main walk turns left, passes Nexo and heads towards the spectacular peaks of the Bernia Ridge. *(Alternative walk 2 turns right here, to return to Tárbena.)*

After descending a little, the ridge disappears from view and the road bears right towards Campana and Aitana. The village of Tárbena is laid out on slopes to the right. At **4h13min** pass a concrete road leading right, to a few yellow houses with orange roofs. Within a minute or two, take an asphalt track (waymarked with blue paint) that goes up to the left and starts by running back above your previous route. There are almond groves to the left and the Bernia Ridge to the right. Ignore driveways to the left and soon descend between some houses, the Binar-real Valley stretching out deep on the left.

As the concreted track takes a sharp left hairpin bend (**4h22min**), go straight ahead on a rough track. Ignore a track going off left at an open patch and, as your track bears right, ignore two more tracks to the left (**4h25min**). Your view now stretches all the way along the Algar Valley to Campana and Ponoch. Pass a house on the left and continue winding downhill, past some ruins and towards the Pas dels Bandolers. A very steep track goes down to the right just before you go under ELECTRICITY CABLES (**4h45min**). In one minute you pass a storage shed on the left and in another minute reach an open junction where there's a small RUINED HOUSE (**4h47min**). (*Alternative walk 1 rejoins here, from the left, and Alternative walk 2 carries on downhill.*) Just *before* the house, take the track off right. Continue straight ahead along the edge of a field (a short stretch has been ploughed up) and join that very steep track as it winds, less steeply, downwards. After passing through groves of avocados and oranges you descend steadily again for some time. Ignore a track off to the right (**5h03min**) and soon pass a *finca* on the right. Meet a narrow asphalt road and follow it past the small reservoir (**5h34min**) and all the way back down your outward route to the CAR PARK at **Casa Federico**.(**6h**).

Looking across the Binarreal Valley to the Serra de Ferrer

13 VALLEYS OF THE SERRA DE AITANA

Distance: 10km/6.2mi; 2h25min

Grade: easy, apart from a steady climb of 300m/980ft during the first 45 minutes; all on good clear tracks

Equipment: see page 42

How to get there and return: 🚍 to Guadalest. Take the C755 west from the village and at the first roundabout go straight on. Almost immediately turn left up a narrow road signposted to El Trestellador restaurant (Car tour 3 at 33km). Pass the restaurant after about 1km and 500m further on reach Font Molí, a small cluster of houses, with the old mill on the right. Turn right at the open area with room to park beside the wooden fence. The *font* and picnic tables are just above you (*P*13a).

Short walk: Font Molí — Guadalest Valley overlook — Font Molí. 4km/2.5mi; 1h20min. Easy climb/descent of 180m/590ft. Equipment, access as main walk. Follow the main walk for 29min, then turn right on a track. It skirts to the left of cultivation, then cuts right through the cultivation to a *casita* (43min). From here the now-grassy track winds up to the right of the house, into another, partially-cultivated valley. Take a narrow path to the left of the cultivation. It becomes a little indistinct towards the end of the cultivation: keep a couple of terraces on your left and wind to the left of a dead tree, to reach the end of the valley (49min). Now climb out of the valley; you will see your path continuing ahead. At 52min you crest the ridge, and the whole of the Guadalest Valley lies before you. Notice, up to the left, the main walk track descending towards some rocks which mark the defile we call 'Chough Gully' — this is your goal. From the edge of the ridge, follow the path slightly left and head downhill, to wind around the top terrace. At 54min you join the main walk track: pick up the notes at the 2h-point, to return to Font Molí.

M uch of this walk is a pleasant stroll through a series of high-altitude valleys, offering a variety of interesting features. Birdwatchers in particular can look forward to some worthwhile sightings. Don't be put off by the climbing on the first stage. Just take your time and enjoy the surroundings.

Start out at **Font Molí**: walk up the road which passes to the left of two picnic benches. Ahead are more benches and, on the left, the *font* (*P*13a). It gives a steady trickle of water, but the main flow is directed down a *canaleta* into the village. Just before the *font,* take a rough path up the hill to the left. Meet a track (**3min**) and turn right, to start your steady climb to the base of Penya Mulero. At **6min** the track forks. The main track goes straight ahead (*P*13b), but you must turn sharp right and pass through a CHAINED GATEWAY. On a bend to the left, at a short concreted section (**13min**), ignore two tracks off to the right. (The second of these is your return route.) On the few flat stretches, stop and admire the views: Aitana rising above you, the Guadalest Valley with its picturesque villages below you, and the coast at Altea in the distance.

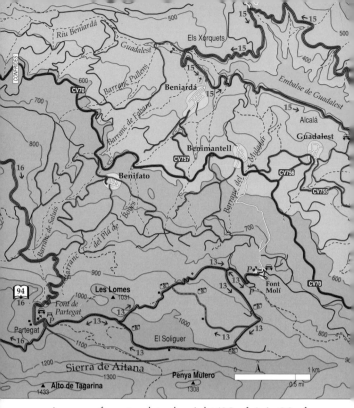

Ignore a farm track to the right (**23min**). In **28min** your track bears right, offering the first views of Penya Mulero — there is no mistaking this huge craggy rock with its sharp pinnacles. A minute later (**29min**), ignore a track going off to the right, down into a small valley *(but turn right here for the Short walk)*. As your track bears right, heading below the cliffs of **Penya Mulero**, ignore a track off left to another valley and up to the main Aitana Ridge (**35min**). In autumn, patches of white and purple heather flourish alongside the usual herbs — but be sure to look up towards the crags. Not only might you have disturbed the noisy resident ravens, but you may be lucky enough to see a golden eagle. Whether stationary, perched on the top of one of the buttresses, or in flight, its size and colour make it unmistakable. Less startling, but worth a mention, are the black redstarts that flit around the bushes, and, in winter, the small flocks of rock bunting.

A saddle with a small hillock on the right and almond groves either side marks the end of the climb (**46min**). Take a last glance back at Penya Mulero and don't be surprised if you flush partridge along the next stretch. Entering another valley, you come upon EL SOLIGUER, a

Approaching Partegat

pretty *casita* not permanently inhabited but still in use (**50min**). Descend gently through groves; after summer rains take care not to tread on the delicate meadow saffron crocuses which push their way through the stony path. Benifató Castle comes into view at the top of a rise, precariously perched on top of a craggy outcrop in the northwest (**1h**).

At **1h03min** you reach a fork. You will later go down to the right, but for now go straight ahead. To your left are the antennas and domes of the military installation on top of Aitana; ahead lies another cultivated valley. Ignore tracks off into the groves; go past a chain between red gate posts (**1h18min**). The track leads down to **Partegat** (**1h23min**), a tiny valley below a spur of Aitana (see photograph above). Here there are a few houses, picnic benches and a *font* (**Font de Partegat**; *P*16), where you can refill your water bottles. *(Walk 16 passes through here.)*

Retrace your steps to the fork and turn left downhill (**1h43min**). As you descend through this high valley listen for the raucous calls of chough and locate them much further down as they fly in and out from the high rocks. The track sweeps round an old ruined *casita* (**1h55min**) and continues downhill with views of Aixorta ahead. The Short walk rejoins from the right (**2h**) just before the track passes between high rocks on either side (we call this narrow defile 'Chough Gully'). Look out also for blue rock thrush and for the deep *nevera* (snow well) alongside the track on the left.

Continue until you rejoin the concreted section of your outward track (**2h14min**). Turn left and retrace your steps, either by descending on the rough path straight down to the *font* or by continuing along the track which leads you more gently to **Font Molí** (**2h25min**).

14 PENYA SELLA

Distance: 7km/4.3mi; 2h10min

Grade: moderate, with an ascent and corresponding descent of about 200m/650ft. A high-altitude walk along a fairly wide ridge (avoid windy days). Despite the lack of a path, navigation is only a problem in the event of mist or low cloud.

Equipment: see page 42; also compass

How to get there and return: 🚌 At the 4.9km-point on the CV770 Sella to Port de Tudons road (the 23km-point on Car tour 4), turn right on a narrow asphalt road signposted to Benifató. Park at the end of the asphalt (6.5km from the turn-off), by the Font Pouet Almany.

This walk offers splendid views and is high enough to blow away all the cobwebs. Short though it is, this is a must for those who enjoy ridge walks.

Begin the walk where the asphalt runs out at **Font Pouet Almany**. A track runs straight ahead here, but take instead the sandy track bending sharp right (at the right-hand side of the *font*), going past a ruined *casita*. Ignore the track up left to the *casita,* but take the next one (about 20m/yds further on), heading for another house. Just before you reach it, two craggy hills appear in front of you. You are making for the saddle between them.

The track, rocky and in poor condition, goes past the HOUSE (**6min**) and then runs out at its upper terraces (**13min**). Make your own way left uphill to the SADDLE (**16min**). From here the mountain views are breathtaking — Aitana to the north and Campana behind El Realet (known locally as 'the Shark's Teeth') to the south. Stretching to the west is the Penya Sella Ridge with a sheer drop to the Sella Valley below. 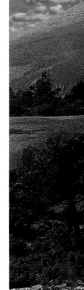 From here to the far end of the ridge there is no obvious path (so watch out for snakes!), but the walking is easy, and there is no danger of getting lost.

Turn right and climb to the FIRST SUMMIT on **Penya Sella** (**31min**). Continuing west, you'll see a couple of cairns. The second marks the second, highest peak (1159m/ 3800ft). From here, descend steeply over smooth rocks and then across the saddle, heading for a third 'peak'. This is in fact a rounded shoulder with twin summits, the first reached at **1h08min** and the second, across another shallow saddle, at **1h 13min**. From here, you will see the ruined house shown opposite (one of the CASAS

Casas de Dalt (1h38min into the walk)

88

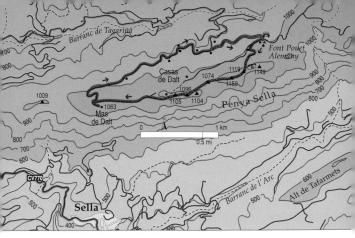

DE DALT), its terracing stretching almost to the top of the ridge. Make your way down to the terraces and ruins.

Take the overgrown track going left from the side of the house and soon meet another track. Turn left and head west on a continuation of the ridge. Ahead you will see MAS DE DALT, a makeshift windsock indicating its use as a refuge by hang-gliders. As you approach this *finca* (**1h35min**), a track joins you from below on the right. You will take this track, but first explore a bit — the house, a well, and the jumping-off spot for the hang-gliders taking the quick route down to Sella!

Return to the junction and go left downhill, a sharp descent. You pass an old *era* (threshing floor) and a few houses (**2h05min**). Meeting the asphalt road, turn right and walk back to the **Font Pouet Almany** (**2h15min**).

15 EMBALSE DE GUADALEST

Distance: 10km/6.2mi; 2h25min

Grade: easy, with just two short steep sections (total ascent/descent 100m/330ft). The paths are good, and you can't get lost.

Equipment: see page 42

How to get there and return: 🚌 to a point between the 2km and 3km markers on the CV755 just east of Guadalest (the 30km-point of Car tour 3). Drive down the tree-lined road, signposted 'Presa de Guadalest'. This takes you to the dam wall. Park in the car park.

Shorter walk: Embalse de Guadalest, south bank. 5km/3mi; 1h30min. Grade, equipment, access as above. Instead of crossing the dam wall at

Aixorta rises behind the Embalse de Guadalest

the start, take the track skirting the southern side of the reservoir. After 31min turn right on a track which descends quite steeply towards the river. Take the little path (44min) down to the pebbly beach at the side of the water (*P*15). Return the same way.

I t is so unusual in this part of Spain to be able to walk close to water for any length of time that we felt this delightful walk should not be omitted, despite the fact that some of it is along the narrow service road around the reservoir. The reservoir is surrounded by mountains, and you will be able to appreciate their grandeur without the effort of climbing them.

Start the walk by crossing the DAM. Aixorta is visible ahead (photograph opposite) and the immense gorge carved out by the Guadalest River falls away on your right. The Serrella Ridge stretches along to the left and, if you look carefully at three trees at the end of the Aixorta Ridge, you will see Serrella Castle, well camouflaged amongst the rocks. Also to the left, Benimantell Castle (or El Castellet) perches precariously on top of a rocky outcrop (from further round the reservoir it looks even more startling). Directly behind you is Guadalest Castle.

At the end of the dam wall, follow the road (marked with superfluous RED DOTS) left along the side of the water. At times it rises above the high banks of the RESERVOIR before falling back down again. At the far end of the reservoir you will see the village of Beniardá, the antennas on top of Aitana and Benifató Castle — another astonishing feat of construction. The road sweeps round what could, in wetter times, be arms of the reservoir but the steep banks are now clad with pines or almond groves and, in more sheltered spots, with *nísperos* (medlars) and a few vines. Added to the calls of Sardinian warblers and whinchats are the calls of the gulls on the water — an unusual sound in this mountainous terrain.

As you join a road coming in from the right (from the direction of Castell de Castells; **56min**), turn left and continue around the reservoir, sometimes in the open, sometimes through pines. Towards the END OF THE RESERVOIR (**1h15min**) you begin to hear the beautiful sound of running water deep in the valley below. The source of the sound becomes evident as you reach a bridge across the sparklingly clear **Guadalest River** (**1h25min**). Before crossing you might like to take a detour up the side of the river just for the pleasure of watching the water running between the reeds and cascading over the rocks, with two small waterfalls nearby.

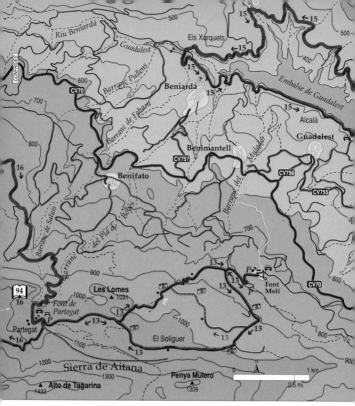

After crossing the bridge the road sweeps round to the left and climbs quite sharply, passing Beniardá's municipal SWIMMING POOL (**1h33min**). About 100m/yds past the pool, turn off left through a GATEPOST bearing a red dot. (The road bears right into **Beniarda** where refreshment is available.) You are now on a fairly wide track leading downhill. Ignore a crossing track and continue heading down towards the river. Reach water level (**1h40min**) and continue on a path to the right, through some pines. A detour on a path going off to the left at this point takes you to the water's edge — a lovely spot for a break.

Return to the main track alongside the river (more red dots). It crosses a little *barranco* coming down from Beniardá and passes through an area of trees and reeds. It then climbs, steeply again, to a wide track running along the SOUTHERN BANK OF THE RESERVOIR (**1h53min**). Take this track. Notice, on the right, a couple of minutes later, a section of an enclosed *canaleta*. Further on, the holes in the steep sandy banks of the reservoir are the nests of bee-eaters. These colourful, migratory birds are unmistakable, and you are quite likely to see them in spring or summer. A leisurely stroll takes you back to the DAM (**2h25min**).

16 THE *FONT* CIRCUIT

See cover photograph **Distance:** 21km/13mi; 5h50min

Grade: Strenuous, with ascents and corresponding descents of 600m/1970ft.

Equipment: see page 42

How to get there and return: 🚌 to Confrides (the 49km-point on Car tour 3). Park in the village. 🚐 to Confrides, if you are staying overnight.

Short walk: Three *fonts*. 7km/4.5mi; 2h06min (being an out-and-back walk, it could be shortened). Strenuous, with an ascent/descent of 300m/985ft. 🚌 to Font de Partegat (the 40km-point on Car tour 3). Follow the main walk from the 2h06min-point to the 3h09min-point at Font Forata and return the same way.

Alternative walk: Benifató Castle. 9.5km/6mi; 3h35min. Access and grade as main walk, with an ascent/descent of 360m/1180ft. You must be sure-footed and have a head for heights. Trekking pole useful. Follow the main walk to the 1h18min-point, then turn right up the stony track towards the castle rock. Turn right at a junction (1h24min) and follow the main track as it gradually winds up closer to the castle. The walls become more obvious, as does the dragon's-back ridge on the southern side. You pass through an open area (1h47min) where the track bends sharp right. Cross a stretch of loose stones (1h57min) and turn up a narrow path through almond terraces. This takes you round the other side of the dragon's-back and steeply up to the castle walls (2h13min). Take great care on this final, quite vertiginous climb. Explore the castle, then return to a fork just before the almond terraces (2h18min). Go right, along the foot of a scree slope. At a junction (2h24min) go steeply down to the right. When you meet a surfaced road (2h29min), turn left and follow it back to Font Freda (3h05min). Retrace your outward route back to Confrides (3h35min).

This magnificent walk is in three distinct parts: a stroll on country lanes with the serras as backdrop; a climb past several *fonts* on a path lined with wildflowers in late spring, coming within touching distance of the summit of Aitana; and a descent on a wild, isolated mountain road. For maximum enjoyment choose a calm day.

Start at the pension/bar EL PIRINEO and walk back below **Confrides** and down the road in the direction of Benifató Castle. Pass a parking area and PICNIC BENCHES and, a minute later (**13min**), turn right on a narrow road signed to the BuenaVista/Eagle's Nest Restaurant. This old road from Confrides to Benifató takes you up past the restaurant to a junction at a house — **Font Freda** (**31min**). Turn left, admire the Serrella ridge, and pass an attractive little house and garden as the gradient lessens. Approaching a CREST (**43min**) Benifató Castle comes into view. A few minutes later, at a junction on a right-hand bend, go straight ahead. The road descends for a while, then levels out, with the rugged peaks of the Bernia ridge in the distance and Aixorta to its left, closer to you. You pass a 30kph SIGN and a little later see Benifató village and Guadalest Castle to the left. Go under electricity cables and head toward the impressive buttresses of Partegat shown on page 87. There are several *casitas* on these slopes, and ahead are the radar domes atop Aitana.

As you contour between almond groves, notice a track going back to the right, with red arrows on the walls (**1h18min**). *(The Alternative walk turns up here to Benifató Castle.)* Carry straight on to a T-junction and turn right (**1h24min**). Soon the long ascent to Partegat begins. Cross a bridge over the **Alfafara** stream then join the road coming up from Benifató (**1h40min**). This leads you to the **Area Recreativa de Partegat**, dominated by the **Casa de Partegat** (**2h06min**). The **Font de Partagat**, stone benches and barbeque facilities cater for almost every need (***P*1**6).

From the parking area go up the stony track signposted to Sella. Pass alongside almond groves *(Walk 13 comes in from the left here)* and, at a junction, turn right on the PR21, signposted to the Port de Tudons (**2h12min**). Your route is now confirmed by PR waymarkers all the way back to Confrides. This track circles above Partegat, then climbs towards the cliff face of Aitana. It soon becomes a narrow path, zigzagging between gorse (cover photograph) and passing through an area of boulders. Leave Partegat behind as the path levels then climbs gradually round the head of the next valley and up to where the domes on Aitana are visible again. Shortly after taking a left fork, you pass a reservoir and *font* (**2h48min**). The path resumes its ascent and, at a T-junction, the summit of Aitana is very close (**2h56min**).

Turn right on a track that undulates below the ridge. Pass a track off to the right and climb steeply once more, to reach **Font de la Forata**, in an open area with a signpost (**3h09min**). A path goes left up to the summit from here, but you continue straight on under Aitana's skirts and through pine woods, to the HIGHEST POINT OF THE WALK (sigh of relief!) at a junction (**3h18min**). Go straight ahead here, and also at the next junction a few minutes later. Before passing directly below the TV antenna, spot a *nevera* on the right.

Now begin the descent (**3h31min**) and admire the wonderful views into the valleys below. As the gradient

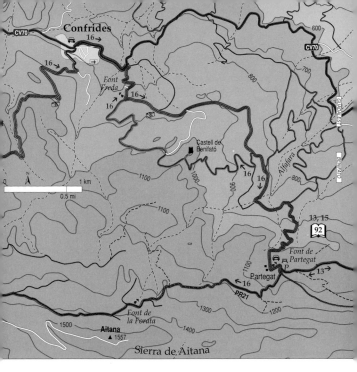

steepens, take it slowly. In late spring the wildflowers here are splendid. You will soon see your next objective set among the terraces below. Zigzag down, taking the final obvious short cut to miss the last long bend and reach the **Mas de la Font del Arbre** (**4h07min**). There are many picnic benches here set amongst the trees.

Continue past the *font* and up the main track, part dirt, part surfaced. It sweeps to the right below some houses and then back left to pass above them. Walk along the top of fruit terraces and a *casita* on the left (**4h27min**). Now in open country, the road turns sharply to the right, facing the Serrella ridge once more. Begin to descend, passing a complex of houses with extensive fruit groves (**4h 45min**). Rise gradually past pines to a white *casita* at a crest (**4h57min**) and then begin the long, winding descent — perhaps accompanied by the wild calls of black chough. The stunning views change at each bend and are worth many pauses on the descent.

Benifató Castle comes into view once more (**5h23min**) just before a sharp left hairpin, then Confrides appears (**5h30min**). The road continues its steep descent through pine woods to a PR-signed junction in **Confrides** (**5h 48min**). Fork left here and sharp left at the next junction, to reach your starting point at El Pirineo (**5h50min**).

17 CAMÍ DE L'ESCALETA AND THE OLD ROAD: CIRCUIT FROM BOCAIRENT

See also photograph page 33   **Distance:** 12km/7.4mi; 3h26min

Grade: moderate ascents/descents of 300m/980ft; no navigation problems, but danger of vertigo on the return

Equipment: see page 42

How to get there and return: 🚗 to Bocairent (the 89km-point on Car tour 4). Park in the old square (follow signs to the Tourist Information Office). *Possible alternative return:* 🚌 from Pou Clar to Bocairent (the infrequent service passes just a few minutes after leaving Ontinyent; check times in advance). Or retrace your steps (add 1h50min).

Short walk: Covetes de los Moros. See description page 98.

The Camí de l'Escaleta is the old mule trail which served the textile factories *(fábricas)* strung out along the Barranco de Ontinyent from Bocairent to Ontinyent. The waters of the *barranco* were used in the preparation of textiles, and mules carried finished bales to the towns. At times the *camí* is stony or well-packed earth, but there are some amazing sections cut from the solid rock — resembling bobsleigh runs! Pou Clar, a lovely *font* with deep pools and picnic tables, is a picturesque spot for a break before returning along the spectacular route of the old Ontinyent to Bocairent road.

Start out at the TOURIST OFFICE in **Bocairent**. Walk up the hill, then down the medieval cobbled road to the restored BRIDGE over the *barranco* (photograph page 33; **6min**). The road sweeps left, passing the village *lavadero* (**10min**) and a *font,* before coming to a collection of houses and a cross, at a junction (**19min**). Take the middle, asphalted road. After the

Approaching the first old mill on the Camí de l'Escaleta

last house on the left take the rocky track up left, beside some CONCRETE POSTS.

Turn right when you meet another track and, at a WALK SIGNPOST (your return route comes in here), turn left and go up a series of little steps hewn out of the rock. This is the start of the **Camí de l'Escaleta**. Deeply pitted from the constant pounding of hooves, the trail takes you almost parallel to a track, then over the side of the hill, to another track. Cross this and locate the continuation of your trail as it descends into the **Barranco de la Luna**.

After the first 'BOBSLEIGH RUN', the **Barranco de Ontinyent** comes in from the left and the first old *fábrica* comes into sight (**56min**; see photograph opposite). The trail bears left, down to the old building, and continues along the *barranco* to a second *fábrica* (**1h04min**), from where it widens to a track. High cliffs, pitted with caves, rise up out of the *barranco,* and terraces adorn the gentler slopes. The *barranco* has been dammed in places near the mills, and deciduous trees line its floor, which you will criss-cross at times.

When the track forks, go left on a path to the third *fábrica* (**1h06min**). Villa Flor, the largest of the mills, is about 100m/330ft long (**1h 15min**). Not far beyond it, a disused *canaleta* winds past the fifth *fábrica* (**1h 24min**). The trail goes under the *canaleta* and skirts the fence of a house (**1h 31min**), before joining its access track. Turn left, pass a HYDRO-ELECTRIC PLANT and reach the MAIN BOCAIRENT/ ONTINYENT ROAD (**1h40min**). The walk turns right

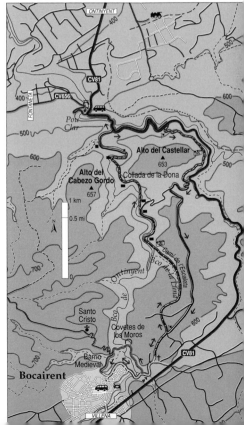

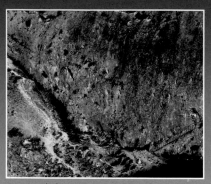

Covetes de los Moros

Short walk: Covetes de los Moros.
2km/1.2mi; 35min. Easy. Access and equipment as main walk. This stroll explores the network of 53 caves shown above. Hewn out of the cliff, they were once inhabited, probably by the Moors. While you can go directly there

and back (signposted from the Tourist Office; 25min return), try this more pleasant, circular route. Follow the main walk to the bridge (6min). A couple of minutes later, before reaching the *lavadero*, take an obvious path going steeply down to the left. Cross a stream

and bear left. The path runs above a couple of caves and descends, to skirt the right bank of the stream all the way to the *covetes*. Metal steps take you up the vertical cliff to the only entrance. After your visit, return to the stream and turn right. Cross the stream just below its junction with a second stream, then strike uphill to the top of a rise. Ahead is the first Station of the Cross leading to a hilltop *ermita*. Make for this but, when you get there, turn left down a wide path. Cross an old bridge and follow a path to a cobbled road, where you turn left and climb back up to the main square (35min).

here but, if you want a break, Pou Clar lies 10 minutes to the left, just after a left turn to Fontaneta — the place to flag down a bus.

The kilometre or so along the road verge is not very pleasant, but it's worth it to make this walk circular. Take care and, at a WALK SIGNPOST on the right (**1h54min**), scramble up the eroded steps and on to a PR-marked path which climbs steeply before contouring (**2h11min**) round the hillsides, home to the uncommon black wheat-ear. Views are magnificent and ever-changing. Join a track (**2h24min**) and within just a few minutes turn left on another track. This takes you up across open hills (where the Camí de l'Escaleta is deep below on your right) and eventually leads into another 'BOBSLEIGH RUN' (**2h43min**).

From here locate white arrows or PR markers at junctions and follow them all the way back to the WALK SIGNPOST of your outward route (**3h04min**). From there return to the bridge and back up to the TOURIST OFFICE (**3h26min**).

18 ALCOI • BARRANC DEL SINC • COLL SABATA • MONTCABRER • RACO LLOBET • MURO DE ALCOI

Distance: 20km/12.4mi; 5h40min

Grade: strenuous, with ascents of 770m/2520ft and descents of 870m/ 2850ft. Mostly on good tracks and paths; navigation straightforward.

Equipment: see page 42; also compass, long trousers, plenty of water

How to get there: 🚌 to the Alcoyana bus station in Alcoi. Turn right along Avinguda l'Alameda (the main road just up from the bus station). Just before a bridge and the tall Alcoy Plaza building (5min), you reach the Mercadona supermarket, where the walk begins. Or 🚗 to Alcoi (the 55km-point on Car tour 4 (page 31). From the Mercadona supermarket (58km), use the *walking* notes on page 101, to park near the brickworks. *To return:* 🚌 from Muro to the first stop past Alcoi's railway station

Short walk: Barranc del Sinc. 2km/1.2mi; 40min. Easy stroll. Access: 🚗 to/from Alcoi (see instructions for motorists above). Follow the main walk from the 25min-point to the 44min-point, then retrace your steps.

Alternative walk: There are many possibilities in the Serra de Mariola, where you can link up Walks 18-20). Two suggestions below:

1 Alcoi — Coll Sabata — Cocentaina. 13km/8mi; 4h20min. Moderate-strenuous, with a climb of 440m/1440ft and a descent of 360m/1180ft. Equipment as main walk, less long trousers. Access as main walk; return by 🚌 from Cocentaina, and walk back to the Alcoyana bus station or your car. Follow the main walk to Coll Sabata (2h). Take the PR37 path straight ahead, signposted 'Talecó de D'Alt', soon passing this ruin. Keep left here, heading across a field towards a slope. The path undulates, then descends steeply to an unmade road, where you turn right. The road narrows to a path and joins another road (2h43min). Turn left towards a quarry on the hillside ahead. Meeting another road by the Refugio de las Foietes, turn left again. Then fork right almost at once for 'Castell, Sant Cristófol'. Cross the asphalted quarry road (2h58min) and head downhill on a track, watching for a 'Castell' signpost, indicating your ongoing path to the left. The path passes above a grand old *finca*, Mas de la Penya, then comes to a delightful spot directly under the *penya* itself — a massive cliff much used by Alcoi's rock-climbing fraternity (3h08min; *P*18c). The path continues to a narrow asphalt road (3h21min). Turn left uphill, past a chain barrier, to reach a crest overlooking Cocentaina Castle. From here take the path down to the left, to the castle *mirador* (3h34min). Now a concrete road leads you steeply down to Sant Cristófol — an extensive *zona recreativa* just above Cocentaina, with a bar-restaurant (3h55min; *P*18b). Continue down the road for a few minutes, then turn right on a narrow path (PR37.1). It crosses the railway line, runs above the industrial area, crosses a track and descends to an asphalt road. Turn right and make for the church. Cross the church square diagonally, then turn right up Carrer Major, a pedestrian precinct. At the top, turn left and left again to reach Plaza Alcalde Reig (4h20min), from where you can catch the bus back to Alcoi.

2 Sant Cristófol — Montcabrer — Sant Cristófol. 17km/10.5mi; 5-6h. Strenuous, with overall ascent/descent of about 850m/2800ft. Access as for *P*18 (page 14). From Sant Cristófol follow the PR37 (path lined by wooden railings) northwest via three *fonts* and Mas de Llopis, then head south via Montcabrer and the GR7 to Coll Sabata, from where you can use the notes for Alternative walk 1 above to return to Sant Cristófol.

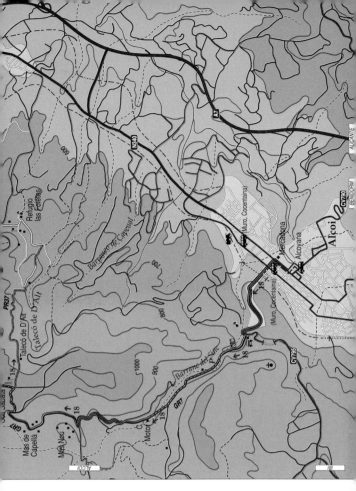

The Barranc del Sinc is a picturesque start to this walk, which takes you over Coll Sabata and across rocky ridges to the summit of Montcabrer (1390m/4560ft). It then descends into the cultivated valley of Racó Llobet and follows another *barranco* down into Muro. It is a delightful walk offering a variety of landscape and views.

Start out at the MERCADONA SUPERMARKET in **Alcoi**. From its front door, cross Avinguda l'Alameda and go up CARRER ISAAC PERAL. This road leads directly uphill into CALLE LA SALLE and then CARRER BARRANC DEL SINC. Pass a *font* and the municipal SWIMMING POOL on the right, then an ELECTRICITY STATION on the left. Continue past the last row of houses to a BRICKWORKS (its chimney is visible ahead; **25min**). Those travelling by car should park near here, and deduct 25min from all times given below. Take the track which heads right, on the bend, at the brickworks.

From here you are looking directly at the cliffs shown opposite — the entrance to the **Barranc del Sinc**. You will see your track winding towards it. The red and white GR7 markers, sometimes faded, will take you all the way to the top of Montcabrer. The track crosses the *barranco* and leads you through the defile and to a path. At about **33min** you come upon a beautiful picnic spot (*P*18a), where the roughly-cobbled path and steps pass close to the watercourse. There will not always be water here, but even when dry it is an impressive spot. Cliffs tower above as the path continues along the *barranco*, crossing from side to side, passing a *casita* with a willow tree (**44min**). *(The Short walk turns back here.)* Now you leave the *barranco* bed, continuing at a higher level through pines which are home to short-toed treecreepers. Ignore a track to the left (**53min**) and continue parallel to the *barranco*, until a steep climb takes you past a water control station ('C Motor' on the map; **1h05min**) to an asphalt road. Turn left. Being a cul-de-sac, the road carries little traffic.

The *barranco* deepens on your left as you climb steeply, eventually passing a LARGE STORAGE BUILDING just before Mas Nou, a little community with one very old house and some new ones (**1h25min**). The road continues round into Alcoi, but you must take the track which goes up to the right, just on the bend. This takes you away from the Barranc del Sinc and up through a pine wood, past a chain barrier, to **Mas de Capellá** and its surrounding terraces (**1h40min**). Pass between the main buildings and turn right to ascend gently through fruit and almond groves and past a couple of sheds. As the track sweeps right (**1h51min**) take the waymarked path to the left and climb through a valley of pine trees to a clearing — **Coll Sabata** (**2h**). Look out around here for Dartford warblers, which are resident on these upper slopes. A track and several paths leave from the col. *(Alternative walk 1 takes the path straight ahead here; Alternative walk 2 turns left.)*

The main walk takes the path up to the left, past an enclosure containing an ANTENNA. *Ignore* the signposted PR37 path to the left (**2h08min**), and fork right uphill with the GR7 over pine-clad slopes where, in autumn, the heather is quite spectacular. Looking back once past the tree line (**2h20min**), you will see Alcoi spread out in the valley below, with the heavily-wooded slopes and *ermita* of Font Roja across to the right. As the path approaches and crosses a shoulder, it becomes quite indistinct on the rocky terrain, especially in snow. However it is clearly marked with very large cairns and GR waymarks. The walking is easy, and the cairns lead you to a small crest (**2h49min**), where a deep *barranco* goes down left towards Font Mariola. You may find it hard to believe that we had to wade through knee-deep snow here one February!

From the crest, look for your continuing path making its way round towards the rocky outcrop of Penyes Monteses, which has a little pole on top. The path is clear for a while and gradually loses altitude. As it drops over the rocks to a lower level, it becomes indistinct for a short time. Keep about 20m/65ft below the highest point of the ridge and look carefully for the GR7 markers. The path soon reappears and leads you round to the left of **Penyes Monteses** (**2h55min**). From there the path is almost level and takes you round to Montcabrer (you can see the craggy summit ahead). At the end of the open stretch (**3h03min**) the crags are directly ahead and, as the path

The walker is a mere dot in the land-scape, below the cliffs which flank the narrow en-trance to the Barranc del Sinc (Picnic 18a).

winds round them to the right, you should leave it: take the little path up left to the SUMMIT of **Montcabrer** (**3h13min**). On returning to the main path, turn left to reach a terrace directly under the end of the crags. This is **Font Pouet**, where you may find a walkers' notice asking you to observe the country code (**3h25min**).

Continue on this path, descending at first gradually and then more steeply. Ignore a turn-off right to Mas de Llopis (**3h38min**; *Alternative walk 2 comes in here*) and reach a SADDLE (**3h44min**) at the top of the slopes above Muro. From here the GR7 goes left towards Font Mariola, but you should ignore this and turn right downhill on a path just a few metres/yards further on. You wind down quite steeply through prickly gorse, before contouring above cultivated terraces and getting your first glimpse of a house as you round a bend. The path circles above its terraces, then descends to a track (**4h**). Turn left, pass the dry **Fuente de Vicente**, and reach the house at **Racó Llobet** (**4h04min**).

Walk to the right of the house on a narrow but clear path which winds right and then left, to a track. Turn right on the track but, almost immediately, turn right again, on a narrow path which runs above the broad terraces and leads to the **Barranco de Puig**. Follow the left bank of this beautiful *barranco* through thick vegetation, with Serrella dominating the view ahead, to a RUINED FARM (**4h25min**). Turn left at the track here; about 100m/yds further on you meet the track coming down from Racó. Turn sharp right and continue downhill to a right-hand bend, just past a huge boulder (**4h35min**). Here take the path on the left. (Both track and path follow the **Barranco de la Cabrantá**, but the path is more pleasant.) Just after passing a *casita* (**4h43min**), rejoin the track as it comes in from the right.

At about **5h05min** you pass the first houses on the outskirts of **Muro**. Cross the railway and continue straight on to the main road (**5h33min**). Turn left towards the petrol station (200m/yds away; adjacent bars, café, restaurant), then cross the road to a roundabout where there are two more restaurants. Turn right at the roundabout towards Muro centre. Catch your bus a few metres/yards along on the left outside a shop, MURELEC ELECTRICIDAD (**5h40min**; no sign, but the bus is used to picking up here). Back in **Alcoi**, alight from the bus at the stop *after* the railway station, then walk down the hill to AVINGUDA L'ALAMEDA and back to the ALCOYANA BUS STATION. Or use the notes at the start of the walk to return to your car (add 25min).

19 THE *CAVAS:* CIRCUIT FROM AGRES

See map pages 100-101; see also photograph and notes pages 6-7

Distance: 16km/10mi; 5h55min

Grade: fairly strenuous, with ascents and corresponding descents of 820m/2700ft overall. The paths and tracks are good underfoot, except one short section along the ridge, where the path crosses rocks and is indistinct. Navigation is straightforward.

Equipment: see page 42; also compass

How to get there and return: 🚌 to/from Agres (the 78km-point on Car tour 4). Park in the village and make your way to the church. Note: It is possible to shorten the walk by 2h and cut out about 600m/1970ft of climb and descent by driving up to the refuge and starting there. Drive up the road towards the *ermita,* but then turn right opposite the third Station of the Cross. ***But be warned!*** This road, although reasonably wide and well-surfaced, *is extremely steep with hairpins as sharp as hairpins can get and its sides are unprotected from treacherous drops.*

Shorter walk: Agres — three *cavas* — Agres. 7.5km/4.7mi; 3h. Fairly strenuous, with ascents/corresponding descents totalling 650m/2130ft. Access as above; equipment as page 42. This out and back hike takes in three of the four snow wells visited on the main walk. Follow the main walk to the 1h27min-point at Caveta del Buitre (1h32min), then return to the refuge and retrace your steps all the way back to Agres.

Alternatives: This walk and Walks 18 and 20 interconnect, so a variety of alternative routes can easily be devised.

This walk takes you up pine-clad mountain slopes, down into a peaceful, sheltered valley and along a ridge with amazing views on either side. *And* there are buildings to explore. In addition to an *ermita* and a *refugio* (mountain hut), we pass four *cavas* (snow wells; see pages 6-7), probably all dating from the 17th century. Such wells were only built in exposed areas, where snowfall was virtually guaranteed — so, even on a sunny day, remember that it could be very windy and somewhat chilly up on this high serra.

Start out in **Agres:** walk up the road to the left of the CHURCH (as you face it). Pass a *font* on the left and look for the Ermita de la Mare de Deu, your first objective, on the hill ahead. Just after a small PLAYGROUND on the outskirts of Agres (**4min**), climb stone steps on the right. At the top, join the road to the *ermita* at the SECOND STATION OF THE CROSS. Turn left uphill, pass the tortuous road up to the refuge, and reach the **Ermita de la Mare de Deu** (**11min**; *P*19). Take the narrow concrete road to the left, in front of the buildings, through the car park. Pass a *font* and take the track straight ahead, behind a CHAIN BARRIER.

The track climbs quite steeply, providing views down into the Agres valley. Close to the ruins of the old convent building, small signs ('Teix' and 'Cava') direct you onto a path going right (**15min**). Ignore the yellow- and white-

Cava Arquejada, sited at 1220m/4000ft, near the refuge, it is elegantly constructed with six gothic arches topping the hexagonal exterior.

waymarked path to the left (**19min**) and continue straight ahead through pines, alongside a *barranco*. You cross this stream (**25min**) just before a path comes in on the left. There are many hunters' paths and short-cuts, but you will have no difficulty keeping to the clear, zig-zagging, main path. As you progress uphill you will see two groups of antennas on the ridge ahead. You are making for the refuge which is between them. When you meet a wide track (**57min**), ignore signs directing you to the right (to the refuge); cross the track diagonally to the left, continuing uphill on a rocky footpath with yellow and white waymarks. Shortly after a pebbly stretch of path, the REFUGE appears just above you (**1h10min**). This refuge (open and manned at weekends and holidays) was built in 1974 on the site of a ruined house, previously occupied by the workers and guardians of the wells. Walk about 100m/yds to the left on the vehicle access road, to look at the **Cava de l'Habitació** — 7m/23ft in diameter and 10m/33ft deep, with a semicircular crypt roof (**1h15min**).

Return to the refuge and continue along the road to **Cava Arquejada** which you can see ahead. It is probably the most beautiful and most visited *nevera* in Alicante. The well itself is fashioned mainly from natural rock and has six upper openings and one lower tunnel opening. Take the road which continues behind this *cava*. In 10 minutes, as it turns left and starts to descend, take a track off to the right, which leads into the small depression housing **Caveta del Buitre** (**1h32min** 'Vulture's Well'; photograph page 7).

Cava Gran, with its massive walls, resembles a fortress.

This well has four access points, and its circular cupola is in excellent condition.

Return to the road and head downwards. Within a minute or so notice a cairn on the right marking your narrow rocky return route. Continue down quite steeply, with views opening up over the whole Mariola valley and to Cava Gran over to the west. At a signposted junction at the gates of **Foia Ampla**, bend right (**1h53min**). In a few minutes, as you round a bend, look up to the top of the ridge ahead and to the right, to locate the circular stone building of the Cava Gran — your next port of call.

Continue along the track past a modern house on the right, with a colourful WELL (**2h08min**). You will see an old *finca* set into the hillside ahead, below the crags of El Portín and the *cava* (**2h11min**). Continue on this main track as it rambles gently downhill, and eventually you will come to a major track crossing (**2h35min**). Walk 20 turns north here, to climb to the ridge above. You do the same, so turn right on the wide but rough track leading over the LOW BRIDGE, and use the notes on page 109 to follow Walk 20 from the 10min-point to the ridge at the 50min-point (**3h15min**). Walk 20 turns left here, but you go right, along the top of the ridge. The path is indistinct in places, but you can't get lost if you keep to the TOP OF THE RIDGE, heading generally east. Come to **Cava Gran** (also called Cava de Don Miguel; **3h27min**). Standing at 1060m/3475ft, its huge size and the thickness and solidity of its walls give it the appearance of a fortress. It is hexagonal, constructed on two levels and has three tunnels. Ruins of the workers' building are close by.

With your back to the main tunnel, go straight ahead, heading east along the ridge (over several small peaks), to make for the next *cava*. The terrain is rocky, and the path is indistinct in places. There are various different routes over the rocks, but if you stay just below and on the right-hand (southern) side of the ridge, you will pick up the main path from time to time. At **4h01min** you come to a small SADDLE from where you have a good view into the valley below. The peak ahead is stepped with rectangular rocks, and the dense undergrowth on the south side is impassable. So climb the few metres/yards to the top of the saddle, and you will see a track coming up through the pine forest below on the northern side. Descend the few metres to the track and turn right, to round the 'stepped' peak and climb back to the TOP OF THE RIDGE (**4h15min**). Then leave the track just before it begins to descend, and take a path on the left; it continues east along the ridge.

Maintain altitude atop the ridge until you meet a wide track, your outward route to Foia Ampla (**4h23min**). Turn up left here and follow your outward route back to the refuge (**4h45min**).

To return to Agres, retrace your outward path from below the refuge. Cross the wide track (**5h**) and zigzag downhill, ignoring tracks off to the right, until you reach the signposted junction (**5h38min**). Turn left and walk in front of the **Ermita de la Mare de Deu** (**5h44min**). Take the road downhill as far as the SECOND STATION OF THE CROSS, where steps off to the right lead you back into **Agres** (**5h55min**).

20 FONT MARIOLA • ERMITA DE SAN TOMAS • EL PORTIN • ALT DE LA COVA • COVA DE BOLUMINI • FONT MARIOLA

See map pages 100-101 and photograph opposite

Distance: 8km/5mi; 2h25min

Grade: moderate, with a gentle ascent of 220m/720ft to the main ridge at El Portín and corresponding descent. Paths are generally good, but overgrown in places — care is needed to locate them.

Equipment: see page 42; also compass, long trousers

How to get there and return: 🚗 to Font Mariola (the 100km-point on Car tour 4). Park in the picnic/camping area.

Short walks (both are easy; access as above; equipment as page 42)

1 Font Mariola circuit. 2.8km/1.7mi; 50min. Follow the main walk to the turn off just before the *ermita* (19min). Turn left, and immediately left again, to walk along the edge of the pine wood and the ploughed field to the campsite visible ahead. Turn left on the asphalt road, and follow it back to Font Mariola (red and white GR7 waymarks).

2 Mariola Castle. 1.6km/1mi; 50min. From the picnic benches at Font Mariola you can see the Moorish castle atop the heavily-wooded hill. Walk up the track (a post on the left is marked with red paint), into the pines. The track becomes a path, for a while following the boundary fence of a *finca* down to the right. After a few minutes it bears left up the hill and leads you to the ruins of the castle. Return the same way.

This delightful walk leads you through the fertile, well-wooded Mariola valley and up onto a sheer ridge overlooking the valley of Agres. You'll clamber up onto the crags at the top of the ridge and walk through some prickly gorse (don't forget the long trousers!) to the site of an early Iberian settlement. Just over the rocky shelf, you explore a massive cave near the sheer cliff face, before descending back into the valley. Font Mariola is an idyllic place to relax and picnic (**P**20) — as long as it is during the week and out of season! You could easily combine this walk with Short walk 2 up to the castle.

The walk starts at the PICNIC BENCHES by **Font Mariola**. Mariola Castle is perched on the knoll on the right, and your track runs below it, heading up the valley through mature pine woods. At a crossroads (**10min**) turn onto a wide but rough track going left over a LOW BRIDGE. The main track going straight ahead (leading to Foia Ampla) is the route used by Walk 19, which joins you at this point. At **19min** a track coming in from the left is your return route. (*Short walk 1 turns left here.*) Continue towards some buildings. On the right is **Mas el Parral,** ahead is the **Ermita de San Tomás** and to the left is a large red brick building.

Opposite: the Mas de Fontanerets from El Portín, with the Agres valley in the background

Mas el Parral, once a magnificent *finca*, is now a beautifully restored hotel, and the surrounding land is private. However, ignore the *'No walkers'* sign attached to the building — it is there to prevent people wandering around the hotel grounds, and the owner assures us that 'proper walkers' are welcome. All she asks is that you respect the privacy of her guests and keep to the main track. Do not be tempted to peer in the windows or wander around the guest facilities, including the swimming pool area and the horse paddock.

Turn left to pass the red-brick building and then follow the track as it bends right, to pass a restored WELL. A few minutes later, just before a right-hand bend with a fenced-in stone hut and lots of standing water, turn left up a rough, muddy track. Look out on the right after about 40 metres for a cairn marking a narrow path. Turn right and follow this slightly overgrown but clear path, to reach a FENCE. The path follows the fence for a few minutes, before forking left and rising about 10m/yds across a loose and rocky surface to a LOW CREST (**34min**).

This is a good spot to take your bearings. To the right (east) is Mas de Abres, with Montcabrer rising behind it. The ridge with the *cavas* (Walk 19) stretches east to north from Mas de Abres, and your next objective — the crags of El Portín — are just ahead of you to the northwest. Turn left on a narrow path which rises, then bears right to run under the crags. In about 10 minutes you reach an open area below a *font.* You can see the crags up to the left, but you go straight on. The path is a little indistinct here, so take care. Bend left at a cairn and walk though low scrub, to meet a clearer path at a small SADDLE (**50min**). *(Walk 19 leaves here, by heading right on the path running along the top of the ridge, to reach Cava Gran in 12 minutes.)* Turn left here, climbing up towards the crags. The path leads under the highest rocks, on the southern side, before winding round to where a short scramble will take you to the SUMMIT of **El Portín** (**59min**).

From here locate, slightly to the south of west, Alt de la Cova, a terraced hill which is the site of an Iberian settlement. It is your next objective. Also locate Mariola Castle to the south. Walk about 20m/yds towards a point between those two landmarks and, below, locate a rather isolated large rock that has a cairn on top. Make for this rock, to join a narrow path heading down in the direction of Alt de la Cova. The path runs along the foot of the wooded slope and then descends, through sometimes

prickly undergrowth, to a track (**1h10min**). To the right
is the *finca* shown on page 108, **Mas de Fontanerets**, but
you must turn left and follow the path to the SADDLE below
Alt de la Cova (**1h18min**). From here several different
paths climb the short distance, through abandoned
terraces, to the plateau; take your pick. The settlement
on **Alt de la Cova** (**1h30min**) dates from the fourth to first
centuries BC, and clear signs of it still remain. Local
museums house many artefacts from the site, and the
whole plateau is worth investigating. Evidence of past
cultivation abounds, and the plateau is so strategically
sited that it is easy to see why it was chosen as a site by
these Bronze Age inhabitants. In the middle of the
plateau there is a small depression, about 10m/30ft deep.
The northern (right-hand) edge of this depression is
edged with a rocky shelf. Near the far end of the shelf
you will see a path going diagonally downhill to the east
(everywhere else there is a sheer drop to the Agres valley
below). This easy path, shielded from the drop by rocky
plates, leads in a few minutes to the massive **Cova
Bolumini**. This cave also formed an important part of the
settlement.

The path does continue past the cave, under the cliff
walls and above a sheer drop, to the Fontanerets track.
But rainfall in this area is relatively high, and the
combination of damp rocks and slippery grass means that
great care must be taken. The more cautious (including
us!) will prefer to retrace their steps up to **Alt de la Cova**
and return to the MAIN TRACK AT THE SADDLE (**1h50min**).
Turn right and continue down towards Font Mariola. The
track descends above ploughed fields, with the
commercial campsite (where there is a bar/restaurant) off
to the right. The *ermita* and Mas de Parral look
magnificent down in the valley to your left. The track
descends between fields, returning you to the track of
your outward route. Turn right and enjoy a good view of
Mariola Castle as you walk past the camping areas, back
to **Font Mariola (2h25min)**.

Distance: 15km/9.3mi; 4h45min

Grade: moderate, with ascents and corresponding descents totalling 800m/2620ft; tracks are good, and navigation is no problem.

Equipment: see page 42; also warm clothing, compass (in case of mist)

How to get there and return: 🚌 to/from Ibi. Alight at the stop on the slip road off the main road in the town centre; this stop is after the traffic lights, where the Centro Optico is on the right. (The stop for your return bus is just opposite.) Cross the road, go back the way the bus came in for about 30m/yds, then turn right. Pass the market and, in 'bank square' (100m/yds further on), take the second exit on the right. A five-minute walk up the hill leads to the main street, with the church to the left. Turn right; the *ajuntament* (town hall, with flags outside), is 100m/ yds away. Or 🚗: park at the *ayuntamiento* (town hall; the 125km-point on Car tour 4).

Short walk: Ibi — Cava Canyo — Ibi. 10km/6.2mi; 2h54min. Moderate, with a climb and corresponding descent of 500m/1640ft. Equipment as page 42; access as above. Follow the end of the main walk in reverse to Masía del Canyo and Cava Canyo; return the same way.

Alternative walk: Ibi — Casa Foiaderetes — Barranco de las Zorras — Ibi. 12km/7.4mi; 3h30min. Moderate climbs/descents of 550m/1800ft. Access and equipment as main walk (no compass required). Follow the main walk to Casa Foiaderetes (59min), then take the track to the right. It winds down past terracing, lusciously green in spring, to a *finca* near the Barranco de las Zorras (Vixens' Gully) (1h15min). As the track begins to climb again, it makes a sharp right-hand bend. Leave it here, on the obvious path which goes straight ahead (1h20min). It follows the *barranco* to a four-way junction (1h50min). This is the 3h08min-point in the main walk. Turn right along the PR-marked path and follow the main walk back to Ibi.

I n the 1960s and 70s the area around Font Roja was scheduled for extensive development but, fortunately, these plans were abandoned through lack of finance. However, it was not until 1987 that environmentalists succeeded in having it declared a Parque Natural. The ecological importance of its mixed woodland and resulting ecosystem will become increasingly evident as you walk through the park. You will also pass several old *fincas* — of some importance in their time, but now abandoned. At the Font Roja complex (*P*21) you can rest and picnic in beautiful surroundings, before undertaking the ascent to Menejador. As you begin to feel a bit chilly or as your legs start flagging as you climb, console yourself with the thought that you are attaining a height just greater than that of Ben Nevis. The return route takes you past three of the park's *cavas* (snow wells), before descending back into Ibi on a delightful old mule trail.

Start out in **Ibi** with your back to the *ajuntament:* walk up the street opposite (CALLE DE SANTA LUCIA, but not sign-

Font Roja (Picnic 21). This walk takes you through its mixed woodland. Above 900m/3000ft the holm (or evergreen) oak, with its dark green foliage, dominates, but the humid north-facing slopes also provide ideal conditions for other species — Valencian oak, ash, and maple. Lower down, the oaks share the land with pine, deciduous trees and shrubs whose leaves, throughout the autumn, provide colourful relief from the monotony of the evergreens. In the past, the yew tree was also present in great numbers, but today only about forty of this species remain.

posted at this end). You are making for the hills you can see at the end of the street. On your left is the more easterly of Ibi's twin hills, this one crowned by the Ermita de Santa Lucia. Notice some steps going up on your right — your return route. *(The Short walk climbs up here.)* Almost at the edge of town you pass to the right of the SOCIEDAD DE PALOMAS DEPORTIVAS (Pigeon Fanciers' Club), with its array of coloured launching boxes. Just before the road sweeps round to the left (**10min**), take the track straight ahead, between two BRICK GATE-POSTS. Here you pick up your first yellow and white waymarks (PR26). Almost immediately, the track turns left, to cross a small *barranco* and climb steeply up the far side. At the top, cross a track and continue straight ahead uphill, towards a SMALL WATER CONTROL BUILDING ('Casa Motor' on the map) and three pines.

The track passes to the right of the building and goes round the head of the *barranco*, taking you to the foot of a steep rocky slope. The path up over the rocks is a bit of a clamber, but it is clearly marked and not difficult. As you reach each waymark, look for the next one above you, so as not to lose the route. On reaching the top of this section (**29min**), you come upon a lone pine tree and can see the continuing path going straight ahead.

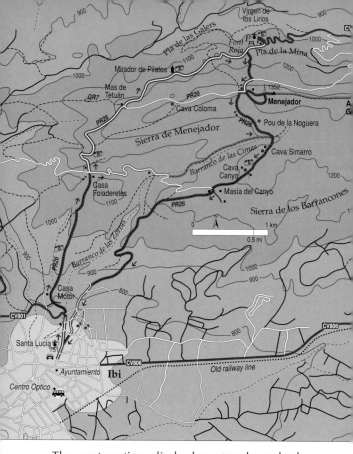

The next section climbs less steeply and takes you through herbs and gorse. Take time to turn and look behind you where, from left to right, you will see Carrasqueta, Penya Roja and the Serra de Maigmó (Walks 23-25), with the coast and *salinas* between them. At **45min** the path narrows and curls round the hillside, gradually gaining height. Ignore a path coming up to join yours from the *barranco* down on the left (**50min**). You pass some almond terraces just before reaching a good spot for a short break — **Casa Foiaderetes (59min)**. The house is in ruins, but its terraces are still tended and there is an attractive well nearby.

As you leave the house a track crosses your path. Keep straight ahead *(the Alternative walk turns right here)*. Your track now rises steeply through a lovely area of mixed woodland, where you ignore a path to the right (**1h10min**; white waymarks) and pass the terraces of **Mas de Tetuán** and then the house itself (**1h24min**). Yew trees still stand beside its old *era* (circular threshing area).

Walk in front of the house and, just beyond it, turn left at the junction, leaving the PR26 and picking up the red and white waymarks of the GR7, one of Spain's long distance footpaths (a similar mark is visible on the stone wall in the photograph on page 113). This is a park track, and will take you to Font Roja. Descend, quite steeply in places, past the **Mirador de Pilatos** on a rise to the left (**1h38min**) — an excellent place for a view down into the valley and up the heavily-wooded slopes of Menejador. Continue straight on at the junction at **Pla de las Galers** (**1h45min**) — so named because the *galer* (Valencian oak) is so abundant here. As you approach Font Roja, look well over to the left, where Montcabrer (Walk 18) rises imposingly. At **Pla de la Mina** (**1h54min**), the little path off to the right is your eventual route up to the summit of Menejador; but, for the moment, keep straight ahead: go down the steps through the picnic/barbecue area at the upper end of the **Font Roja** complex (*P*21). The information centre is then just off to the left (**2h**). Further down are the large **Santuario de la Virgen de los Lirios**, toilets, and another picnic/camping area with views to Alcoi and Montcabrer.

From here retrace your steps to Pla de la Mina and turn left up the stepped path (marked with a camera sign and yellow arrow) which climbs steeply to meet another park track. Turn right to a SADDLE (**2h30min**) just below the summit of Menejador. Here there is a junction of tracks and a large stone-clad WATER TANK. Do the round trip (little more than 10min): walk up the path, past the building and the antenna, to the SUMMIT of **Menejador** (1352m/4435ft). (If you want to conquer another summit, a path leads eastwards to **Alto del Ginebra**, about 10min away.) On your return, take the track past the WATER TANK, but turn left immediately (**2h43min**), on the PR26 path. It descends steeply past an old stone WELL (**2h53min**) and then levels out. You come to the first *cava* — **Pou de la Noguera**. This large open cavern is 12m/40ft deep and just as wide.

The continuing path undulates above the left bank of the **Barranco de las Zorras**, and you can see it going up the slopes on the opposite bank. Fork right (**3h06min**) and cross the *barranco*, where a path comes in from the right (**3h08min**). *(The Alternative walk rejoins here.)*

Go straight up the other side to **Cava Simarro** (**3h 13min**). This 18th-century structure, the largest *cava* in this area, used to be the most beautiful, and has been partially restored. Above it are the ruins of a *casita*, but you should walk round the *cava* and up the slope, to a crest. From there you can see Ibi down in the valley, as well as the tiled roof in Arabian style of the well-preserved **Cava Canyo**, which you reach at **3h18min**. This is the smallest of the *cavas;* beside it are the ruins of the Casa Nevater ('Snowman's House').

From here the path widens to a rough track and heads towards **Masía del Canyo**, a *finca* in a small cultivated valley. As you approach it, you join a track coming in from the right. Go past the house and its *era* (**3h28min**). You are now on a wide path which passes along the top of the terracing, and heads down towards Ibi. Ignore minor hunters' paths; keep to the clear main PR26 trail. You will realise from the still-visible hoof prints that this zigzag path, at times sculpted out of the rock, is the old mule trail down to Ibi from the *cavas* and the *finca*. Descend past almond groves until you join an asphalt road on the outskirts of town (**4h20min**). Follow the road past a metal fence and between terraces. Keep straight on, then go down steps to join your outward route to the TOWN HALL in **Ibi** (**4h45min**).

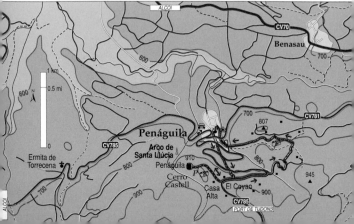

22 PENÁGUILA CASTLE

See map opposite   **Distance:** 6km/3.7mi; 1h53min

Grade: easy, except for the steep climb (230m/750ft) to the castle; one faint path which needs careful location

Equipment: see page 42

How to get there and return: 🚌 to/from Penáguila (the 41km-point on Car tour 4); park in the village.

Short walks (grade, equipment, access as above). Follow the main walk to the **crest** and back (2.5km/1.5mi; 1h08min) or to the **castle** and back (3km/1.9mi; 1h30min). You can shorten both of these walks even further by driving to El Coyao; the 37km-point on Car tour 4): pick up the main walk at the 25min-point.

This walk, largely on pleasant paths, is short but well worthwhile. Penáguila Castle, with its origins in the 8th century, was reputedly a stronghold of the great Moorish leader Al Azraq. There have been some restorations over the years, but little now remains of the ruins. However, standing at the base of its walls, one can appreciate the strategic importance of its position.

The walk starts in the MAIN CHURCH SQUARE in **Penáguila**. Facing the church, leave the square to the right. Go through a second square diagonally to the right, then head left up the main street, CARRER VERGER DE PATROCINI. When it bears right, go straight ahead up some WIDE, SHALLOW STONE STEPS. Cross the main Alcolecha road and take the concrete road going up the hill. It climbs very steeply before crossing the Port de Tudons road (**5min**) and joining a narrow path about 10m/yds to the left. It runs alongside a small olive grove. This pretty path, with all the appearances of an old Moorish trail, climbs in zigzags, crossing the road twice more. Behind you, to the east, there are magnificent views of Serrella and, on the cliffs below the castle, many caves have been formed by the erosion of the soft rock.

The path ends as it joins the road once more (**24min**). Turn right and, on the first bend, reach the gates of **El Coyao** (**25min**). Take the little path that goes up to the right of these gates. Ignore paths off to the left and keep climbing, as you wind around the Penáguila side of this hill, **Cerro Castell**. The narrow path is eroded in places. At a CREST (**34min**; **P**22) the ruins of the castle come into view, a large cross towering above them. From here the surrounding serras are spectacular, while Penáguila paints a pretty picture in the valley below. From here locate the indistinct path which descends to cross the rocks of the small saddle, below the ruins of an old tower. Take care as you pass the TOWER, and clamber up a steep

117

path to the rest of the ruins of **Penáguila Castle (46min)**. Explore as you wish and then retrace your steps to the asphalt road at **El Coyao (1h05min)**.

From here you can either return along your outward route (turn left and walk back to your outward path, then follow it downhill to the left) or, for more variety, continue on the road to the first hairpin bend to the left **(1h15min)**. Here a track goes straight ahead towards a small *casita* and some groves. Follow this track as it winds up through the groves. At **1h20min** an overgrown track can be seen going off to the left through pines. Follow this to a little path going right, some 20m/yds further on. Being indistinct, the first part is waymarked, but it soon becomes clear as it leads you down through pine woods, beside a *barranco*. After a steep section, you meet another path **(1h28min)**: turn left and round the head of the *barranco*. Across the valley you will soon see the village of Benasau, nestled under the end of the Serra de Serrella; below on your right, a track comes up from the village of Alcolecha. Your path passes above terraces and approaches, but does not meet, this track. The path eventually becomes a rough, rocky track as it descends towards Penáguila. It passes under the old AQUEDUCT seen below as it crosses a *barranco* **(1h46min)**. It then crosses the Penáguila-Alcolecha road and continues through the **Jardí de Sants** (a 'historic garden') and leads to some steps on the left. These take you up into **Penáguila**. Turn left up a narrow street and reach the CHURCH SQUARE on the right **(1h53min)**.

You pass under this old aqueduct on the return to Penáguila.

23 LA CARRASQUETA: PORT DE LA CARRAS-
QUETA • POU DEL SURDO • MAS DE LA
COVA • PORT DE LA CARRASQUETA

Distance: 14km/8.7mi; 3h55min
Grade: moderate, with ascents/
descents of 280m/920ft on good
tracks and paths; navigation easy
Equipment:
see page 42,
Dog Dazer
**How to get
there and re-
turn:** 🚌 or
🚐 from Ali-
cante to the
Port de la
Carrasqueta
on the N340 (the 144km-point on
Car tour 4)
Short walks (equipment as page
42, access as above)
1 Pou del Surdo. 2.8km/1.7mi;

45min. Easy ascent/descent of
75m/250ft. Follow the main walk
for 23min; return the same way.
**2 Port de la Carrasqueta — La
Sarga — N340.**
9km/5.6 mi; 2h
40min. Easy; as-
cents of 180m/
590ft; descents
of 280m/920ft.
Follow the main
walk to La Sarga
(2h30min), then
go directly to
the N340 (less than 1km away),
where you can catch a bus back to
the Port or to Alicante.
*Photograph: Pou del Surdo
(Picnic 23a)*

With the starting point at 1024m/3360ft, this walk
offers splendid panoramic views for a minimum of
effort. The variety of terrain, from rugged hilltops to gentle
cultivated valleys, and the wealth of interesting features
to be seen en route, ensure enjoyment all the way. Several
properties in this area have dogs, some loose. Take a Dog
Dazer if that worries you (see page 43).

Start out at the *mirador* on the right, at the top of the
Port de la Carrasqueta. Locate a rocky path going along
the ridge from the car park. It takes you under ELECTRICITY
CABLES (**5min**) and joins a track, which soon splits. Take
the right fork; it reduces to a rocky path (**10min**) which
passes beneath a lone pine. From here you have a
fantastic view down into the Xixona valley to the right.
Walk through low, aromatic vegetation and pass a couple
of large cairns, one with an old IRON CROSS on it. The **Pou
del Surdo**, an old snow well at 1100m/3600ft, is a perfect
picnic spot (**23min**; *P*23a). This well-preserved cylindrical *pou* (fenced off for safety reasons) is over 11m/36ft
in diameter and roughly as deep. An iron ladder runs
down the inside wall, and there is a mechanism for
drawing up water.

From the *pou* the wide track will take you to some
ANTENNAS (**28min**) and open up views to the left over the
heavily-cultivated valley, with La Sarga at the far end.
Follow the track as it passes the antennas and undulates,
gradually gaining height. In this area you might disturb

partridge, and you will surely see and hear the thekla larks. Ignore side tracks and climb to a junction (**45min**). Take the track off left, up an embankment, and continue to gain height. We have seen golden eagles soaring over the valleys to the right. At the end of the ridge, a few metres/yards up to the right of the path, is the highest point on this branch of the **Carrasqueta Ridge** (**1h03min**). It is only a minor peak (1224m/ 4015ft), but on top there is a cairn and a clump of Valencian oak trees. Surrounding views are impressive: the high peaks of Aitana with its antennas and Campana with its notch to the east; Cabeço d'Or to the southeast; Montcabrer, Alcoi and Cocentaina Castle (Walk 18) to the north. Continue on the same track, now badly eroded. Descend steeply, before contouring round to the saddle at the end of the ridge (**1h19min**). Climb past the head of a *barranco* on the left and, at about **1h26min**, before reaching a crest where there are two hunting signs, strike off left over open ground, to pick up the parallel track you can see about 100m/yds away. Turn left on this new track and head down a spur, with *barrancos* on both sides. Ignoring side tracks, descend gradually through Valencian oaks, high above the Sarga valley. As you emerge from the trees (**1h56min**), there is an open field to the left and a track going to the right.

Fork slightly left, passing **Mas Plans de Baix**, a farm on the right. Wind round the edge of its fields to a fork (**2h03min**), where you keep right, through pines. Descend to the fields at the far side of the *mas,* and turn left on a wide track (**2h06min**). Caves over on the rocky hillside to the right (**2h14min**) house prehistoric paintings. On the left are the twin horns of the Carrasqueta Ridge. Reach an asphalt road at **Mas de la Cova** (**2h20min**); the house is now uninhabited, but its terraces are still well cultivated. This is a good spot for a break (**P**23b) and you can walk up to the caves.

Then walk down the road, cross the stream bed, and climb the road straight ahead. *(But for Short walk 2 turn right to the N340.)* The road skirts to the left of the tiny village of **La Sarga** (**2h30min**). As you leave the houses behind, fork right on a dirt road. Then fork left (**2h36min**) on a track; at first it runs parallel to the track you just left, then it bends left between fields and through pines, up to a house (**2h46min**). Take the narrow path to the right of the house and continue past a small *casita* and a *lavadero,* up to a *font* in an open picnic area amongst some trees. Join the track behind the *font* and turn right. Pass **Mas Els**

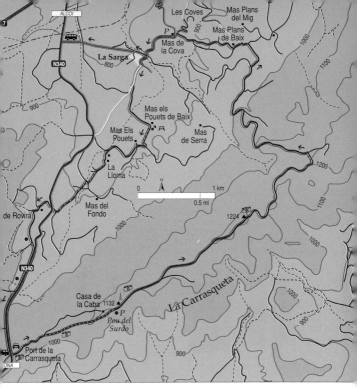

Pouets (**2h53min**) on the right, a farm with its own pretty chapel and attractive surroundings (the chained dogs are quiet!). Continue straight on to **La Lloma**, a collection of attractively-restored buildings. Go round past the front of the buildings (to the left) and climb a track, past a storage shed and through pines, to a three-way fork. Take the left-hand path and continue above the terraces to a T-junction (**3h09min**), where Mas del Fondo is signposted to the left. Turn right here, then go left immediately on an old trail. As you pass under ELECTRICITY CABLES, cross a farm track and climb through trees. Go right at a fork (**3h15min**) and walk through some green gates, to the N340 (**3h20min**).

Cross the road diagonally to the right and go up the track past the fairly extensive, but ruined, **Mas de Rovirá**. The track winds up around terraces before settling in a direction parallel to the road. It descends to road level at a semi-cylindrical *pou*, still used as a well. A track continues past the *pou* but, when it sweeps right, you must head straight ahead across the open ground that borders the road. When a metal fence forces you down to the roadside, cross the road if you wish and continue for about 300m/yds, past another, enclosed *pou* on the right and back to the **Port de la Carrasqueta** (**3h55min**).

24 ELDA • L'ARENAL • CAPRALA • RAMBLA DELS MOLINS • PETRER • ELDA

See map on reverse of touring map   See also photograph page 2

Distance: 18km/11.2mi; 5h (15.5km/9.6mi; 4h10min for motorists)

Grade: easy but long. Good tracks throughout; straightforward navigation

Equipment: see page 42

How to get there and return: 🚌 or 🚐 from Alicante to/from Elda railway station. By 🚗 take the exit from the A31 north of Elda (the 46km-point in Car tour 5). Coming to a roundabout, turn sharp right, doubling back the way you have come, then quickly turn right under the slip road (see map on reverse of touring map). Park on the open ground close to three tunnels. Pick up the walk at the 40min-point.

Short walks (both are easy; equipment as above)

1 Rambla dels Molins. 1.6km/1mi; 35min. 🚗 Drive from Petrer or Elda to Restaurante Molino la Roja (the 94km-point on Car tour 5). Follow the main walk down the *rambla* from the 3h14min-point to the picnic spot (***P***24) — or as far as you like. Return the same way.

2 L'Arenal. 6km/3.7mi; 1h56min for those using public transport; 2km/1.2mi; 36min for motorists. Follow the main walk to the 58min-point and return the same way. Access as main walk.

Alternative walk: Elda to Castalla via the GR7. 19km/11.8mi; 5h20min. Moderate (ascent 600m/1970ft; descent 440m/1440ft). Equipment as above. Access: 🚌 or 🚐 from Alicante to Elda railway station. From Elda station, follow the main walk to the 2h23min-point. This is also the 2h28min-point on Walk 25. Take the GR track up to the left and follow the waymarks to Castalla (Walk 25 in reverse). In 4h50min you will reach the car parking point for Walk 25 and come to the bus stop in Castalla in 5h20min. *Note:* Just before Casa de Angel, a ruined hamlet above Castalla, you could take a very picturesque alternative route into Castalla by following Alternative walk 25-2 via the 'forgotten finca' shown on page 15. This would add about 30 minutes to your total time.

This is a lengthy, but mainly flat walk between serras. Its two major points of interest are a huge inland sand dune and the Rambla dels Molins — a watercourse dotted with the ruins of many old mills.

The walk starts from the main exit of **Elda** STATION: turn right into CALLE GALICIA. Go straight ahead on the main road, under the RAILWAY LINES. Cross the road immediately and locate some steps going down into CALLE RIO SEGURA. At the end of Calle Río Segura, scramble down the bank to the riverside and turn left along the canalised **Río Viñalopó (6min)**. After going under a BRIDGE and across a rough section, you must make a detour round a *casita* and enclosure (**15min**). From here the water is channelled underground and giant reeds grow in the bed. When the path runs out (**31min**) climb up a couple of terraces to the left and make for a small building close to the *autovía*. This bears red and white GR7 waymarks, which you will follow for some time. From here the river sweeps left

The locals claim that L'Arenal is the only inland sand dune in Europe. It is certainly an unusual sight, a rocky hill with one side completely covered in sand.

under a road bridge, but you must take a track going right. You will see THREE TUNNELS ahead: go through any of them, under the *autovía* and up to a crossroads (**40min**). This is the parking place for motorists.

From the crossroads take the narrow waymarked asphalt road. Pass a long AQUEDUCT; then, when the road forks right at a WHITE WALL (**48min**), take the road straight ahead, and fork right a couple of minutes later (where the asphalt runs out). Pass between houses with market gardens, almond and olive groves, and come level with the sandy hill shown above — **L'Arenal** (**58min**; *Short walk 2 turns back here*). There's an information kiosk here, but only open in the 'season'. From L'Arenal a rough, rocky track takes you into the serras. The GR waymarks are always present, if widely spaced. Skirting a wide *barranco*, you pass between the **Serra del Cavall** on your right and **Cabezo del Pino** on your left. At a house (**1h11min**) ignore a track going up to the Serra del Cavall. At **1h23min** ignore another track to a collection of houses. You reach an open area with tracks leading down into quarries; then, from the top of a rise, the mountain valley around the hamlet of Caprala opens out to the left.

At a junction of tracks next to a ruined *finca* (**1h34min**), take the track going down left. Cross the *barranco*, then resume the gentle climb into **Caprala** (**1h45min**), where the track becomes a narrow asphalt road. Follow it through the first part of the hamlet, which is mainly holiday homes, until another asphalt road goes obliquely right, down towards a bridge just below you. Follow this down, cross the BRIDGE, then go straight ahead on another road, ignoring a turn to the right. You pass to the right of a VILLA (**1h58min**) where you will see the well shown on page 2 (although it has since been re-tiled). As the road finally leaves Caprala (**2h04min**), cross a *barranco*, pass a 'VÍA PECUARIA' (pedestrian way) sign and, where the road sweeps left, go straight ahead on a track (another 'VÍA PECUARIA' sign). This badly eroded track climbs through a narrow *barranco* for a few metres/yards. At the head of the *barranco*, you round a DAM WALL and join a broad track. Just after this (**2h09min**) ignore a track off right (PR waymarked) to the Casa de L'Avaiol below the Serra del Cavall. Your (GR) track goes straight ahead, passing to the right of a large *finca* and cluster of houses.

Continue straight ahead, ignoring side-tracks. But not far beyond the last building, at a junction (**2h23min**), ignore the PR143 track to the right. Follow the track in a bend to the left then, at the next fork, leave the GR by forking right. *(Walk 25 comes in here, and the Alternative walk heads left uphill here with the GR, following Walk 25 in reverse.)* Continue on the yellow/white waymarked PR143 as it bends to the right; ignore minor side-tracks. With pines on the left and groves on the right, you come to a crossing of tracks (**2h39min**). Go straight across on the PR143, now in open terrain with far-reaching views to Despeñador and the Serra del Frare in the east. As you round a right-hand bend, look left (southeast): beyond some deep and wide terraces, you can see the end of the Serra del Frare plunging dramatically into the Pantanet Gorge (Walk 25). Your track becomes a narrow asphalt road; it passes some houses in (**Casas de Villaplana**) and meets another road coming in from the left (**2h53min**).

Descend this quiet road through agricultural land. The Serra del Cavall is still on your right. When the main road goes right towards Petrer (**2h59min**), keep straight ahead. After passing a house on the left, the asphalt gives way to rough track. Ignore a track going left to a second house . In spring there are all sorts of wild flowers here, and the resident serins are particularly noisy. The track joins an asphalt road at RESTAURANTE MOLINA LA ROJA (**3h14min**).

Walk a few paces past the restaurant, then descend the yellow/white waymarked PR6.9 into the **Rambla dels Molins**, a mainly-dry river bed. It carries some water in winter and is liable to flash floods after wet weather — *take care!* Walk 25 continues from here up the *rambla*, but your route lies downstream to the right; so make your way into the river bed and enjoy a spectacular walk down to Petrer. The *rambla* is named after the water mills which used to grind the grain grown on surrounding terraces. Ruins of these mills remain alongside the *rambla*, and as you pick your way downstream — beside the watercourse or on a path along one of the banks — it is easy to imagine yourself in the past, leading your mules down this well-trodden route. As a path leads you left around the first of several (usually dry) waterfalls, don't stray up the track going left; take the path back down to the river bed. Cross it and continue along the opposite bank. The setting is spectacular as you walk under steep, sandy cliffs, with oleanders growing along the river bed (**3h30min**; *P*24).

Cross an asphalt road and continue along the water-course. The geological formations are fascinating, as well as spectacular, with mainly sandstone on the northern, sunny side of the gorge, and a variety of much harder rocks on the southern side. A track enters from the right opposite a partially-restored MILL (**3h39min**). Behind it, other buildings are wedged into the hillside, some built into the cliff face, and a tunnel goes through the rock. Unfortunately it is all fenced off.

Another *rambla* comes in from the left where there are almond groves in the river bed (**3h44min**). From **3h53min** an asphalt road runs on the left parallel to your route. About five minutes after passing under some pipes, you enjoy an astonishing glimpse of Petrer Castle ahead. When the castle is in full view, reach an asphalt road (**4h08min**). Turn right and climb steeply uphill. Meet the PETRER-CATI ROAD (**4h13min**), turn left and continue down to a major junction just before the *autovía* at **Petrer** (**4h24min**).

If you parked by the TUNNELS, turn right uphill here (signposted to Aguarrios) for 100m/yds, then take the minor road left. This goes along the eastern side of the *autovía* (don't go under it to the left) and leads back to your car (**4h50min**).

Those taking the bus or train should walk under the *autovía* and to the right of the CARREFOUR PETRER. At the roundabout, go straight ahead — all the way down CALLE DEL MAESTRO ALBENIZ. Cross over and walk down the tree-lined path to the CEMETERY. Skirt to the right of the cemetery, then take a track straight ahead, across open ground. The main road is 50m/yds off to the right: join it and continue past another hypermarket, to a set of traffic lights at another large CEMETERY. Turn right downhill to a roundabout. Cross the road and take a minor asphalt road down towards the river and a SPORTS COMPLEX. You will see two bridges. Head left, cross the river on the SECOND BRIDGE, and clamber up the bank to CALLE RIO SEGURA, ascending the steps at the end. In front of you is a railway bridge: turn left to the bus stop, or go under the bridge and turn left to **Elda** STATION (**5h**).

25 CASTALLA • FERMOSAS PLATEAU • PANTANET GORGE • CATI • DESPEÑADOR • CASTALLA

See map on reverse of touring map; see also photograph page 15

Distance: 31km/19.2mi; 8h50min (add 1h if travelling by bus)

Grade: strenuous, with ascents and corresponding descents of 1045m/ 3430ft. Mainly on good tracks, with only one or two rough sections. Ideal for a balmy winter's day (make an early start!). From April to October, it will probably be too hot to attempt the full walk, so we have split it into three Alternative walks, each lasting about 4 hours.

Equipment: see page 42; also compass and plenty of water

How to get there and return: 🚗 from Alicante to/from Castalla (the 76km-point on Car tour 5). Follow the touring notes (page 37) to the fork at 78km and go right. Park 300m further on, where a road goes right. Or 🚌 to/from Castalla. Alight in Avinguda Onil, at a bus shelter. Continue along Onil for about five blocks, turning right at a red Xorret de Catí sign into Calle Manuel de Falla. Turn right at the T-junction, first left into Dr Fleming then left again into Avenida de Petrer,heading towards the crags of Despeñador. Fork right at about KM1.5, leaving the Catí road; fork right again some 300m/yds further on, on a road. The walk starts here, 30min from the bus stop in Castalla.

Short walk: 'Forgotten *finca*'. 6km/3.7mi; 1h40min. Access by 🚗 as above. Easy ascent/descent of 200m/650ft; equipment as page 42. Follow the main walk to the three-way junction (25min) Take the track furthest to the left; then, 5min later, turn right by a small building. Continue to the *finca* (*P* symbol on the map; *P*25a). Return the same way.

Alternative walks

1 Castalla — Elda. 16.8km/10.4mi; 5h20min. Fairly strenuous (climb 440m/1440ft; descent 600m/1970ft). Equipment as page 42. 🚌 from Alicante to Castalla; return by 🚌 or 🚂 from Elda station. See notes above to walk from the bus shelter in Castalla to the starting point (30min). Then follow the main walk to the 2h28min-point, where you go straight ahead on the GR7. This is also the 2h23min-point on Walk 24. Use the map to follow Walk 24 in reverse, from here to Elda station.

2 Castalla — Casa de Angel — 'forgotten *finca*' — Castalla. 8km/5mi; 2h36min (add 1h if travelling by bus). Moderate (climb/descent 410m/1345ft); equipment, access as main walk. Follow the main walk to the junction just after Casa de Angel (1h05min). Turn left up this rocky track. Climb to a crest, then descend into a dip (1h25min). Here another track goes downhill to the left, through thick pine woods. (From here you could take a 2h return detour to the summit of Despeñador: just continue along the ridge, enjoy the breathtaking views, and return to this point to continue.) Pick up the main walk notes at the 7h39min-point, to descend past the 'forgotten finca' and return to Castalla.

3 Frare Ridge and Pantanet Gorge. 9.8km/6mi; 4h05min. Fairly strenuous, with climbs/descents of 500m/1640ft overall; you must be surefooted and have a head for heights. Equipment as main walk. 🚗 to/from Xorret de Catí (the 86km-point on Car tour 5, page 38). Pick up the main walk at the 5h38min-point and follow it to the 5h54min-point. Here continue left (signposted to the *mirador*), below sheer cliffs. Some 25min after setting out, fork right up to the *mirador*. From there climb a steep narrow path up to the right (clear PR32 waymarks). Then clamber on all fours up through a rocky cleft to a crest (40min; photograph opposite). From here a path leads right to the highest point on the Frare Ridge (1211m/3970ft; 5min away) and on to Despeñador (a further 25min).

Alternative walk 3 is a spectacular hike, only recommended for the agile and vertigo-free. It traverses the long, narrow, crescent-shaped Frare Ridge rising between Elda and Castalla (a different Frare Ridge, near Biar, is climbed in Walk 26). Set out on an April morning, when the valleys are alive with the call of the cuckoo.

But you should head *left.* Just after descending a little, the path comes close to the cliff edge, with fine views over El Cid and the Catí Valley (48min). Soon you see the complete ridge stretching out, with Pantanet Gorge at the far end. The narrow path goes all the way along the edge of the cliff, past several posts and giant cairns. The route is PR way-marked from the opposite direction, so you will not notice the markers unless you look back. But you cannot get lost! The ridge is narrow, the drops are sheer, and you are going all the way to the gorge. As you approach the end of the ridge (2h18min), begin to descend over bedrock. After passing the last cairn, locate a PR waymark on the rock on the right (north) side of the ridge, and another on a tree (both facing downhill). With your back to the tree, facing due west, start descending, keeping to the bedrock. There are more waymarks on the descent and, as the bedrock finishes, you will also see waymarks below in the gorge. Reach the gorge at a walkers' signpost and a *canaleta* (2h36min). This is the 4h09min-point on the main walk; pick up the notes and head left — through the gorge, past the Catí *ermita* and back to Xorret de Catí.

This extra-long walk covers part of the long-distance GR7. You follow wooded mountain tracks and then a rocky river bed through a deep gorge, to a spectacular dam. A country hotel provides a pleasant watering spot before you cross a high peak to return. Botanists will delight in the huge variety of wild flowers and plants to be seen in this area, particularly in spring.

Start out at the junction outside **Castalla**: follow the road (red and white GR waymarks) uphill through olive and almond groves, towards the serra. Fork left on a track (**4min**), cross a stream and pass **La Rambla**, an enclosure on your left harbouring a motley collection of deer, barbary sheep and peacocks. Pass the last of the obvious houses ('FAM, FUM Y FRET'; **15min**), where the road

127

becomes a track. You have good views over the plain of Castalla to the left. Note a track going towards a quarry and an OLD LIMEKILN to the right about 100m/yds away. Then pass two ruined houses, each one with a kiln. The track sweeps round to the right at a THREE-WAY JUNCTION (**25min**). The track on the far left here is your return route *(and the route of the Short walk),* but you go right following the GR waymarks. Pass the chained track to an abandoned *finca* on the right (**30min**). Steep crags rise above. At **53min** come to a faded sign to Finca Fermosa, and a chain across the road. Walk behind the chain and continue to the top of the serra. The ruins of a *finca*, **Casa de Angel**, are on the right (**1h**); the terraces are still cultivated. This whole plateau is known as **Fermosas**.

As you continue on the track note a WELL down in a field on the right. The track off left just past this well (**1h05min**) leads along the ridge of the Serra de Maigmó to Despeñador; it is your return route. *(Alternative walk 2 heads up left here.)* Continue through woodland across this high plateau, with the Serra de l'Arguenya on the right. All the buildings up here are abandoned, but the plateau is still heavily cultivated. The GR7 forks right at a junction (**1h16min**), but you go *left.* (The GR inexplicably goes round two sides of a triangle, rejoining your track from the right at **1h26min**.) Ignore side-tracks as you begin to descend from the Fermosas plateau. The valley below opens out to the west, with views as far as the salt marshes beyond Elda, and to all the serras stretching out in the distance. At **2h06min** a short-cut path down to the right cuts off a bend, but the main track is easier walking.

A track crosses yours as you reach more open terrain and the incline lessens (**2h13min**). The prominent flat top and twin peaks of El Cid dominate the skyline to the south. You are now walking through land belonging to the *finca* **Costa o Novayal**, visible on your right. Ignore tracks to the left and right. Two small cylindrical stone constructions are visible in the fields on the left. You pass under ELECTRICITY CABLES by the second of these; a collection of buildings and a *finca* are ahead. After passing a chain barrier, but before reaching the first building, you come to a junction (**2h28min**). Turn left. *(Alternative walk 1 bears right here on the GR7, and Alternative walk 24 comes in here, en route to Castalla.)*

The next section of the walk is common to this walk and Walk 24; pick up the notes for Walk 24 at the 2h23min-point (page 124) and follow them to the

RESTAURANTE MOLINO LA ROJA (**3h19min**). Below the restaurant is a river bed — **Rambla dels Molins**.

Walk 24 follows this downstream to Petrer, but you turn left, upstream, walking on the flat rocks of the river bed for a short while. The *rambla* does contain some water throughout the winter, and after heavy rain there can be flash floods — so be aware. When you reach an asphalt road (**3h29min**), turn right, up towards Catí. The road sweeps round to the left (**3h38min**); then, just before a hairpin bend to the right, climb a track up right past **Casa de la Loma**, a small *finca* where the dog may still be cunningly-chained (we could only just get by out of its reach!). Just before the house, above you on the left, there is a fine *era* (grain-milling slab) and a millstone.

The track, now little more than a path, continues up the hill alongside almond groves and meets the asphalt road again (**4h**). Cross the road and locate a path, slightly to the left, with PR waymarkings; it leads through a pine wood. (There is a wider track going downhill alongside these groves, but your path begins to the right of this track and slightly higher up.) This path leads you into the spectacular **Pantanet Gorge** which you saw from the Casas de Villaplana. Turn right and make your way over the rocks and up through the gorge, passing a signposted path coming down the rocks on your left, on the far side of a *canaleta* (**4h09min**). *(Alternative walk 3 comes down here.)* At the end of the gorge a huge DAM WALL towers above you (**4h16min**). It is an easy clamber up the rocks to the left, to join the continuation of the path; it takes you back to the asphalt road (**4h20min**).

This road continues left uphill to Catí, 3km away. But you must go right for about 300m/yds. Just opposite the entrance to CASA PANTANET, take the PR143 path to the left; it will take you up to the **Coll de Moros**. It's a steady climb up to this ridge, with lovely views of the craggy Serra del Frare to your left. Meet a track coming up from the valley on your right (**4h51min**) and turn left along it. It continues the gentle climb, then levels out. Pass a signposted footpath coming in from the right, before reaching the **Ermita de Catí** (**5h18min**; *P*25b), a lovely spot for a break. From the *ermita*, there are wonderful views across to El Cid and the Serra de Maigmó to the south and east.

Leaving the *ermita* on the same track, you come to a junction: fork left downhill, passing the CASA DE LA ADMINI-STRACION off to the left, with a fine example of a *cava* nearby (reached by track at **5h29min**.) Your track heads right and then turns right, joining a poorly-surfaced asphalt road to a modern hotel with excellent facilities — XORRET DE CATI (**5h38min**).

From the hotel, take the asphalt road west towards Petrer, but after 100m/yds turn right towards the Mirador de Catí, on a wide track with PR waymarks. The crags of Despeñador tower above, as you climb steadily. Ignore side-tracks, including the one to Casa de la Coveta on the left. But when the track sweeps round to the left (signposted to the *mirador*), take the narrower track straight ahead (PR waymark; **5h54min**). *(But go left for Alternative walk 3.)* Fork left (**6h01min**) and, at a T-junction 200m/yds further on, turn left again on another track. This track curls round to an asphalt road, where you turn left. After about 100m/yds you will reach a crest, the **Coll del Portell** (**6h19min**), where there is a brick WATER DEPOSIT. Take the path up left alongside its fence; a steady climb brings you to the ridge (**6h34min**). Turn right to the SUMMIT of **Despeñador** (**6h40min**). The views are among the most spectacular we have seen in all of our walks in Alicante, with about 30 serras being identifiable. It is absolutely breathtaking on a clear day.

Follow the clear track off the summit, initially going west and then northwest along the ridge. A track joins you from the right (from the Catí-Castalla road; **7h11min**). Ignore paths down into the valley on your left. When your track begins to drop sharply into a dip, in a small clearing (**7h39min**), look for a narrower, eroded track going down to the right and take it. *(Alternative walk 2 comes in here from Casa de Angel.)* At at fork (**7h49min**) go left. About six minutes later take a track running obliquely left; it contours round some terraces and suddenly reveals the old but substantial *finca* (**8h**) shown on page 15. As it is so secluded and not named on any maps, we call it the 'FORGOTTEN FINCA' (*P*25a).

Just before the *finca* was a track off right, alongside terraces. Take it now. Rough and rocky, it becomes a path which descends alongside a *barranco*. It widens out again and, at a junction near a *casita*, joins another track. Just before joining this track, turn left on a path going up behind the *casita* (**8h20min**). The path soon becomes a track and meets your outward route at the THREE-WAY JUNCTION (**8h29min**). Turn right downhill, past the LIME-KILNS, to your starting point outside **Castalla** (**8h50min**).

26 SERRA DEL FRARE

Map on reverse of touring map

Distance: 10.5km/6.5mi; 3h15min

Grade: moderate, with ascents and corresponding descents of about 500m/1650ft; navigation straightforward throughout (yellow/white waymarked PR155)

Equipment: see page 42

How to get there and return: 🚌 to Biar. From the 70km-point on Car tour 5 take the exit for Castalla and Biar and follow Biar signs through the roundabouts. As you approach Biar, and just after the 8km road marker, drive downhill following a 'Villena' sign. Turn left uphill at a large 'Bar Restaurante La Corona' sign. Keep heading straight up to the top of the hill, where you meet a forestry road. Park in the open space on the right.

Short walks: The Biar Nature Association has established three botanical trails in the Serra del Frare; all start at the 10min-point in our walk. 1) A short 2km trail, marked in green and primarily for schoolchildren, runs west past the Casa del Frare and ends about 500m further on. 2) A 5km-long trail marked in blue follows our walk, then heads northwest from the Alto del Redondo, back to the Casa del Frare and the start. 3) A 7km-long trail, marked in red, follows our walk, heads northwest past Cova Roja, visits the summit and returns as our walk.

Longer walk: PR155 from La Mare de Déu. 15km/9.3mi; 4h30min. The PR155 'officially' starts at the Santuari de la Mare de Déu de Grácia, east of Biar (see map). You could follow it from there and back.

A major summit, a lovely old trail, and fantastic views all contribute to the magic of this walk. Located in one of the cooler parts of the region, the almond trees blossom later here than elsewhere, making this a perfect walk for a warm day in mid-March.

There are several ways of shortening the walk, and the red trail mentioned above is our favourite. By the time you use this book, many of the plants along the nature trails should be labelled (if only in Spanish and Latin) — among them the thyme, juniper, helichrysum, rock rose, kermes oak, and buckthorn which support the fauna of the Serra del Frare.

Start the walk at the PARKING PLACE by going up the the forestry road and round a hairpin bend. The junction where a track comes down from the right (**10min**) marks the starting point for the green, blue and red nature trails. You will return this way, but for now keep ahead on the track until the PR (as well as red and blue) waymarks point you right, up to the top of **Alto del Redondo** (**40min**), with its fine views. The blue trail heads northwest from here, but the PR and red waymarks lead you zigzagging down a beautiful old stone-laid mule trail, **El Comptador**.

Touching on the forestry track again, follow the

131

waymarks to the right, to **Cova Roja**. (The red-way-marked trail heads northwest from here, at first via a pebbly barranco and then beside it on a rocky path, to the Fonteta de Sant Joan and on to the summit of Frare.) The yellow/white PR155, our route, short-cuts the track, then rejoins it for another 2km, passing the **Font del Destallador** about halfway along.

Just after a zigzag bend, follow the yellow and white waymarks up to the right, to gain the ridge path. From the SUMMIT and TRIG POINT on the **Serra del Frare** (1042m/3420ft; **2h10min**) you enjoy fine views to the left across the heavily-cultivated Biar Valley and to the right over the Sax Valley.

You meet the red path again here, heading directly back to the start. But first follow the PR down to the **Fonteta de Sant Joan** (unfortunately locked on our last visit). The route then rises northeast to a CREST, where you follow the track to the right, descending past some interesting old stone distance markers to a junction (**3h**). Here there is an antenna alongside the fairly extensive ruins of the **Casa del Frare**, and a good view down into Biar, overlooked by its prominent castle.

Take the right-hand track and reach the forestry road of your outward route, where you turn left and head back down to your PARKING PLACE (**3h15min**).

On the red-waymarked trail

BUS AND TRAIN TIMETABLES

The main bus company in the Benidorm area is ALSA. Its website (www.alsa.es), in English, does have timetables for all its services, but it's not very user-friendly.

l'Albir–Benidorm; Bus N° 10; daily; journey time 25min
Departs l'Albir every half hour at 25 and 55 minutes past the hour.

El Trenet ('Lemon Express') narrow gauge railway Alicante–Dénia; daily*

Alicante	0600	0800	1000	1300	1500	1700	1900
Benidorm	0708	0908	1108	1408	1608	1808	2008
Calpe	0737	0937	1137	1437	1637	1837	2037
Dénia	0817	1017	1217	1517	1717	1917	2117
Dénia	0625	0825	1025	1325	1525	1725	1925
Calpe	0707	0907	1107	1407	1607	1807	2007
Benidorm	0736	0936	1136	1436	1636	1836	2036
Alicante	0842	1042	1242	1542	1742	1942	2142

*There are also trains at intermediate times which do not cover the full route

Alicante–Benidorm (Avenida Europa) (ALSA bus company)
Regular service, about every half hour in both directions from Monday to Friday, about every hour at weekends and holidays.

Benidorm (Avenida Europa)–Calpe–Dénia (ALSA bus company); daily except where stated. Journey time 30mins to Calpe; some buses continue to Dénia (1 hour more).
Quite frequent; the first buses depart Benidorm:

Mon-Fri	0740	0830	0915
Sat	0815	1020	
Sun	0815	0955	

Ask about return times when you buy your tickets.

Benidorm — Finestrat; Bus No 14 from Rincón de l'Oix. Journey time 35min
Departs *Mon-Fri only* at 0915, 1115, 1315; returns 1215, 1615, 1815

Benidorm—Confrides (Avenida Europa) (ALSA bus company); weekdays only
Departs Benidorm 1415, arrives Confrides 1600; returns the following morning; check time on the bus.

Calpe—Cala Calalga: Bus No L1 (note that bus L2 also goes, but continues to Moraira)
Departs Calpe railway station 0908 and every hour until 2008; the bus stops at the ALSA office four minutes later (0912, etc) and in the Plaza Colón four minutes after that (0916, etc)

Departs Cala Calalga (outside the Apartamentos Geminis) 0938 and every hour until 2039

Alicante–Alcoi, via Xixona and the Port de la Carrasqueta (Alcoyana Bus Co); see also the next timetable (Alicante–Alcoi via Castalla)
Departs Alicante (passes the Port de la Carrasqueta 40min later)

Mon-Fri	0800	1000	1130	1300	1400	1630	1800	2100
Sat	0800	1130	1330	1630	1800	2100		
Sun	0800	0900	1330	1600	1800	2100		

Departs Alcoi (passes the Port de la Carrasqueta 20min later)

Continues overleaf

Looking towards Ponoch from the 2h10min-point in Walk 4

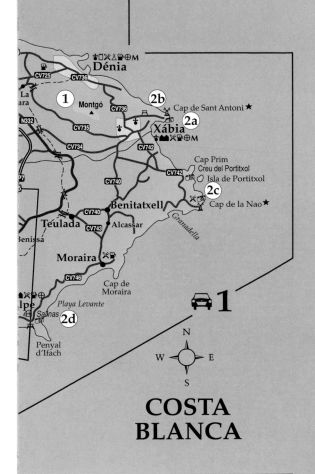

COSTA BLANCA

8 km	
5 mi	
(autopista)	
geway (autovía)	
road	
ad or road in town	
-1600 ft)	
m (1600-3300 ft)	
m (3300-4000 ft)	
m (4000 ft)	
car tour and number	
the walk and number	

🏨	Hotel
✕	Restaurant
⛽	petrol station
⛪	church
★	tourist attraction
■□	castle.in ruins
M	Museum
⊕	medical centre
⊼	picnic tables
📷	viewpoint
△	campsite
∩	cave
⬤	motorway/dual carriageway junction

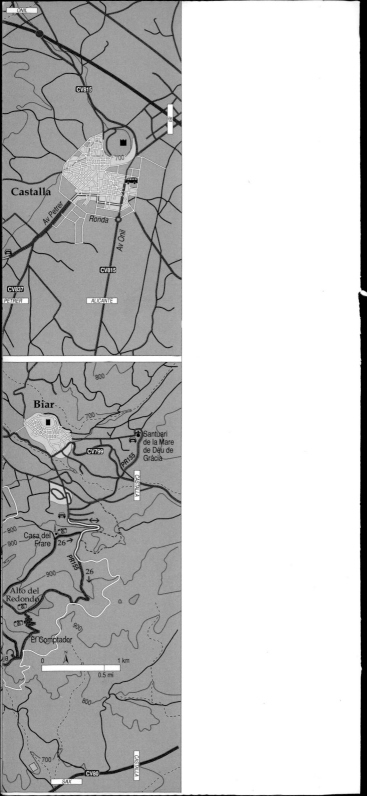

ONIL

CV815

BI

Castalla

700

Av Petrer

Ronda

Av Onil

CV815

CV837

PETRER

ALICANTE

800

Biar

700

Santuari
de la Mare
de Déu de
Gràcia

CV799

PR155

CASTALLA

800

900

Casa del
Frare

26

PR155

900

26

Alto del
Redondo

900

El Comptador

N

0   1 km

0.5 mi

800

700

CV80

CASTALLA

SAX